"This new book, *Transforming Anger,* is excellent. Refreshingly simple and easy to read, the book offers profound insights into the most critical issue of our day: our violence toward self, world, and other. Surely the work is pertinent to our times and fills a serious personal-social need."

> —Joseph Chilton Pearce, author, *The Crack in the Cosmic Egg, Magical Child,* and *The Biology of Transcendence*

"In these days when both health professionals and the public are apt to turn to medication whenever anything goes wrong, *Transforming Anger* is a welcome breath of fresh air. Here is a technique and scientifically-based method for developing self-control that does not short-circuit normal biological regulatory processes."

> —Karl H. Pribram MD, Ph.D. (Hon. Multi), distinguished research professor, Georgetown and George Mason Universities; professor emeritus, Stanford and Radford Universities, author, *Languages of the Brain* and *Brain and Perception;* and coauthor, *Freud's Project Reassessed and Plans and the Structure of Behavior*

"*Transforming Anger* points out that this powerful negative emotion can not only affect our health, but also impair our ability to think and reason clearly. I have been teaching the tools discussed in this new book since 1997. These tools, proven effective in breaking the cycle of anger and all of its consequences, are extremely easy to learn and are based on elegant scientific research that has taught us how the heart and the brain communicate."

> —Bruce C. Wilson, MD, chairman, board of directors, Heart Hospital of Milwaukee, former director, University of Pittsburgh Heart Institute

"How much energy do you waste being angry during your average day? What effect does that have on those you care about? In *Transforming Anger*, Doc Childre and Rozman give you a series of easy-to-learn, highly effective tools and the science behind them, showing you how to prevent that loss of energy and heal those relationships. A much needed fix for our fast-paced, often overwhelming lives."

—Lee Lipsenthal, MD, medical director, Lifestyle Advantage and The Dean Ornish Program for Reversing Heart Disease

Transforming Anger

The HeartMath Solution for Letting Go of Rage, Frustration, and Irritation

Doc Childre • Deborah Rozman, Ph.D.

Foreword by Matthew McKay, Ph.D.,
author of *When Anger Hurts*

New Harbinger Publications, Inc.

Publisher's Note

Distributed in Canada by Raincoast Books

Copyright © 2003 by Doc Childre and Deborah Rozman, Ph.D.
New Harbinger Publications, Inc.
5674 Shattuck Avenue
Oakland, CA 94609

Cover design by Lightbourne Images
Text design by Michele Waters

ISBN-10 1-57224-352-X
ISBN-13 978-1-57224-352-1

New Harbinger Publications' website address: www.newharbinger.com

20 19 18

30 29 28 27 26 25 24 23

FSC
www.fsc.org
MIX
Paper from
responsible sources
FSC® C011935

This book is dedicated to all those who have tried to control their anger but can't. It is also dedicated to people who want to help others transform anger and reinstate care and harmony in life's interactions. Through genuine connection with your own heart's intuition, you can stop payment on personal power loss due to anger, frustration, and blame. This progressively ensures more peace, quality, and happiness in your life, the lives of others, and your environment.

Contents

Acknowledgments

Transforming Anger is the product of over thirty years of research into the human heart. It has been validated by scientific studies on the heart-brain-body communication system. We want to honor those researchers who are bringing new understandings of the intelligence of the heart into science and helping to develop the new field of neurocardiology. We want to thank everyone who has contributed to this book through their scientific studies or through their practice of the techniques and tools presented here. They have proved that it is possible not only to control anger but to transform anger into caring and effective action. We also want to thank those individuals who contributed their transformative stories for this book. (Their names have been changed to protect their anonymity.) We appreciate the health-care professionals who use these tools to help their patients transform anger when nothing else works and they feel hopeless.

We also want to thank their patients and all those who are trying to help themselves and others transform anger using the HeartMath methods.

Finally, we thank Institute of HeartMath researchers Dr. Rollin McCraty, Director of Research, and Dana Tomasino, assistant researcher, who contributed to the editing of this book, and the HeartMath staff for their sincere practice and help in the refinement of these tools. We also thank Priscilla Stuckey for her editorial assistance. We especially thank Matt McKay, founder and publisher of New Harbinger Publications, for inspiring this book based on his care and sensitivity to a need for "in-the-now" solutions in the field of anger management.

Foreword

This book marks a significant breakthrough in the treatment of anger. That's because it is based on a new technology for changing our inner lives. All great new discoveries have roots that run deep in the past. In the same way that the Wright brothers drew inspiration from Chanute and Da Vinci, Salk from Pasteur, and Jung from ancient symbologies, Doc Childre has drawn on a three-thousand-year tradition of recognizing the heart as a source of wisdon and power to create a radically new treatment for emotional problems.

Childre's HeartMath is an extraordinarily effective, easy-to-learn path to personal peace. What makes HeartMath unique is that a few hours' investment in its scientifically researched techniques can offer a level of emotional healing that was previously reserved for longtime practitioners of the major heart-based disciplines (meditation, yoga, Qi Gong, etc.).

These disciplines, recently introduced into modern psychology, have been helpful for some, but HeartMath has added extraordinary new techniques to quickly access your heart and intuition—even in the middle of life's daily challenges.

What initially drew me to HeartMath was the impressive scientific support for its effectiveness. Childre and his associates have sponsored important research that shows the technique's usefulness in reducing blood pressure, coronary symptoms, stress symptoms, depression, and anger reactivity, while improving concentration, productivity, and learning ability. HeartMath can do so much, you'd think Childre was selling snake oil. But he has proved his claims. Over and over. Cardiologists, psychotherapists, and educators have been forced to take notice. HeartMath really works. And it works with amazing speed.

Let me focus now on the subject of this book. As a specialist in anger management, I have struggled with a fundamental problem in all our treatment methods: Angry people are so physiologically aroused that they tend to forget all their therapy and training each time they face a provocation.

The anger management treatment most widely used today relies on a combination of relaxation and *cognitive behavioral therapy* (CBT) or *cognitive relaxation coping skills* (CRCS). These are considered "best practices" for helping people cope with or manage anger. The goal of cognitive therapy is to help you become more conscious of situations that trigger anger, more aware of how you evaluate those situations, and more aware of your emotional, physical, mental, and behavioral responses to those situations. It also provides tools for changing your behavior.

Many anger specialists teach relaxation techniques to help you calm down as you visualize anger-provoking scenarios. During the anger scene, you learn to use coping thoughts to reframe your perspective and change your reaction. The problem is that people who have a lot of past history with anger — who have put a lot of emotional investment into that anger — have imprinted a pattern on their brain that's hard to change. How they see those past situations seems right. They might get a new perspective during a therapy or self-help session, but when the anger-triggering situation comes up again, the old imprinted pattern and the same old anger take over.

It often takes a power stronger than just relaxation or cognitive techniques to change these old patterns. It takes the power of the heart.

What does this mean—the power of the heart? Researchers John and Beatrice Lacey (1970) showed that the heart's nervous system relays important information back to the brain. The Institute of HeartMath took this revelation a step further to discover an extraordinary reciprocal relationship between heart "intelligence" and higher cognitive functions. They found that negative emotions create jagged and disordered heart rhythms, which in turn trigger increased levels of emotional distress. Conversely, people who learn to generate balanced, coherent heart rhythms find themselves far more balanced emotionally.

HeartMath gives you tools to slow down your emotional reactions so the old patterns and anger reflexes stop controlling you. And it opens you to a whole new attitude toward people—and life itself. This book will teach you methods, such as the Freeze-Frame technique, that will give you the power to literally change how your heart beats. With that power, you will also be able to change how you feel and react to the world. Old, angry patterns will begin to melt away, replaced by a sense of appreciation and compassion. And a deep intuitive wisdom.

The HeartMath solution will change your anger at its root—the incoherence in your beating heart. Then it will free you to feel a sense of harmony you've known only in the rarest moments.

In the field of anger management, we've sought for a long time a way to simultaneously relax the body and calm the mind. But it has eluded us. Until now. In this book, Doc Childre and Deborah Rozman will give you a proven way to end the seething and the inner chaos. A way to see through the slights and hurts and irritations. This is the way of the heart. With surprising ease, it will change your life.

—Matthew McKay, Ph.D.
Author of *When Anger Hurts* and
The Anger Control Workbook

chapter 1

Why This Book Is Different

The car in the next lane suddenly speeds up and pulls in front of you, and you have to jam on the brakes to keep from hitting it; your heart pounds and a few well-chosen swear words escape your lips. A few hours later a coworker keeps making the same mistake in file after file, and your patience nears the breaking point. That evening your spouse, for the umpteenth time, won't hear the plea you're making for more time together, and your frustration and resentment build.

Every day, all of us face situations like these, and when we do, we often flare up and get angry. Feeling anger isn't wrong. Anger is a natural human emotion that can stimulate us to take action. Anger is one of nature's ways of enabling people to ward off a threat or attack. It can also be a normal response when we lose basic trust in others, because that too threatens our security and survival.

While anger can motivate us to cope with life's adversities, unmanaged anger leads to feeling out of control. Anger is a powerful energy that can take over your body and brain and make you feel like exploding, but instead you may stuff that energy inside. Then someone can say something unrelated or look at you the wrong way, and you believe they're out to get you. All that stored anger comes bursting out like a volcano. Anger and its fierceness can be frightening to other people and even to you.

The problem is not anger; the problem is that we don't understand what to do with the *feeling* of anger, or understand what is underlying that feeling. Anger can be a place to hide from deeper feelings of insecurity, guilt, hurt, disappointment, embarrassment, jealousy, or resentment. These deeper feelings often determine whether the action we take when we feel angry is effective or something we later regret.

If you are dealing with anger you can't quite seem to manage, this book will give you new hope. It will provide you with new tools to achieve the transformation of anger that you've always wanted but couldn't accomplish.

Managing Anger

Hundreds of self-help books and therapies are on the market to help people manage stress and control anger. There are many good programs. You may have tried relaxation or breathing techniques, time-outs, cognitive reframing, prayer, counseling, group therapy, and other anger coping methods. But if you're like millions of people, no matter what you've tried, you haven't been able to pull off anger control that lasts. There are important reasons for this, and you don't have to feel bad about it. People are wired differently. Perhaps you find it hard to remember cognitive techniques in the heat of the moment; you get blocked and your mind goes blank. Or you may feel that there are so many different anger-management tools you could use that you jam up inside and finally wear out from trying. We know how hard you have worked to control your anger.

We know you probably have felt terrible about your anger at times. It may have hurt your relationships or your job or your health and cost you dearly in terms of your own happiness. Whatever you've tried before, you'll find the methods in this book effective and easy to use. They are effective because they come straight from the heart—your heart. You can use these methods by themselves or to enhance the power of other techniques you have found helpful. You can even use them to unlock creative potentials in other areas of your life.

This book will give you some of the missing ingredients to understand anger in yourself and others. It will show you how to connect with an inner reservoir of untapped power to accomplish what you couldn't before, and do it more quickly than you may have thought possible. *Transforming Anger* is based on solid new science with a lot of evidence and studies to support its effectiveness. You will find stories of people just like you who used the simple, scientific methods in this book not just to control rage, frustration, or irritation, but to get rid of them. You'll see why many have said, "Finally, something to really help with anger."

Technology of the Heart

Transforming Anger is based on *inner* technology that takes you deep inside your heart. It gets your heart, mind, emotions, and nervous system in sync. This inner technology, called the HeartMath System, was developed over the course of thirty years and validated with twelve years of scientific research at the Institute of HeartMath, a recognized leader in stress and performance research and interventions.

Scientists used to think that emotions were purely mental expressions, generated by the brain alone. We now know that this is not true; emotions have as much to do with the body as they do with the brain. Furthermore, of all the bodily systems, the heart has been found to play a particularly important role in emotional experience.

In this book, we provide a model of emotion that includes the heart—together with the brain, nervous system, and hormonal system—as a fundamental component of a dynamic, interactive network from which emotional experience emerges. We show you how to access this network to change your emotional experience.

Over the past twenty years, neurocardiologists have firmly established that the heart is not just a muscle but also a sensory organ and a sophisticated information encoding and processing center. The heart has its own internal nervous system, called the "heart brain" (Armour and Ardell 1994). It enables the heart to sense, learn, remember, and make functional decisions independent of the "head brain."

In the early 1990s, breakthrough studies at the Institute of HeartMath revealed a critical link between emotions and the rhythms of the heart. This research provided evidence that the physical heart is part of the emotional system and that the heart plays a large role in how we feel and think (McCraty, Atkinson, and Tomasino 2001). Most of us intuitively understand this. Poets, philosophers, and religions have said this for ages. But it's only since the advent of modern technology that we've had the ability to see on a computer screen, in real time, how the rhythmic pattern of our heart changes as our feelings change. This gives us a window into the heart.

The next breakthrough at the Institute of HeartMath was discovering how ordinary people can easily learn to shift their heart rhythms and bring their emotions quickly into balance. As they do so, a remarkable thing happens. *Their feelings and perceptions change.* They break free of old emotional patterns.

The brain operates as a complex pattern-matching system. It builds a set of patterns in our neural architecture based on previous experiences, then looks for a match or mismatch to that experience (Pribram and Melges 1969). In 1996, Tiller, McCraty, and Atkinson found that emotions are reflected in the patterns of heart rhythms. Disturbing emotions (such as irritation, frustration, and anger) lead to a more disordered and *incoherent* pattern. On the other hand, positive emotions (like appreciation, care, compassion, and love) lead to a more ordered and *coherent* heart rhythm pattern. The brain monitors and interprets the heart rhythm patterns. It compares an incoming pattern from the heart to patterns it has already stored, and often triggers an emotion based on a pattern match. For example, if you are used to getting angry, an incoherent heart rhythm pattern will tend to trigger anger as a familiar response to incoherence.

Researchers have found that tools and techniques that allow you to shift your heart rhythm into a more coherent pattern enable the brain to find a match to a more positive feeling. Love and related positive emotions not only increase coherent heart rhythms, they also increase *synchronization* between the heart and brain, resulting in improved mental clarity and cognitive performance (McCraty 2002b).

The heart provides a unique access point from which anyone can regulate many of their reaction patterns. Learning to control your own heart rhythms gets to the heart of anger control. It is self-empowering and self-transforming. It gives you access to an internal source of power and intelligence which you probably have tapped into only unconsciously or intermittently. The heart is so powerful—generating sixty times the electrical amplitude of the brain—that it can draw your brain, nervous system, and emotions into its coherent rhythms and unlock more of your own innate intelligence.

The HeartMath techniques in this book will show you how to bring the rhythms of your heart into more coherence on demand. As you practice these techniques, you will have more "aha!" experiences of understanding and mental clarity. The HeartMath methods work for anyone who uses them sincerely. Adults with a long history of anger, children who are easily frustrated, teenagers with shifting emotional moods and raging hormones—all have used the power of the heart to change their feelings and their perceptions right in the middle of an angry reaction. Many are surprised at how quickly the HeartMath tools and techniques work.

As you practice the HeartMath solutions, you learn to love and care in an intelligent and new way. You don't get walked on. You don't become naive or cave in to others' demands. You become clear and centered, and see what's best for you and others. Deep in the heart, everyone has this type of centered love, but it takes practice to connect to it. You start to see life not in an overly idealistic way, but in a realistic and hopeful way.

Intelligent Love

The quickest way you can shift your heart rhythms into coherence is to feel more love and care. So how do you do this? You add love. Not the mushy kind of love you might be thinking of, but a different kind of love. An *intelligent* love that has a businesslike or commonsense quality at the same time. You do this by shifting to an attitude of appreciation, care, or compassion. Or by just making a sincere effort to center yourself in the heart and hold the attitude of love.

Transforming Anger asks you to become an intelligent lover. It asks you to add the intention to love right in the middle of irritation, frustration, or rage, because that's what gets your system back in sync. You have that capacity to love inside you, waiting to be accessed. It's your inner attitude that makes the difference. So learning how to shift attitude right in the moment—when you feel that mechanical dart of anger, that surge of adrenaline, or even while tempers are flaring—is where *Transforming Anger* begins. The HeartMath tools will show you how to access your heart, shift your attitude and perception, and then see a bigger picture. You will come to understand your anger in new ways and have the power to transform it.

The goals of *Transforming Anger* are for you

- *to better understand how and why anger occurs in your daily life*

- *to understand how your body triggers anger and responds to anger*

- *to learn and use fast-acting tools and techniques to get into coherence and release anger*

- *to find and act on new solutions for situations involving anger*

With practice of the tools and techniques, you can transform your anger for good. You can learn how to engage the power of your heart to change your body's responses to stress. Through the power of your heart, you will find self-generated new hope for letting go of rage, frustration, and irritation. The power to understand and transform your anger is inside you if you'll dig in and find it. Using this power is one of the most important gifts you'll ever give to yourself. It creates a paradigm shift in helping yourself. It explains why a change of heart changes everything.

chapter 2

Why Are We So Mad?

In today's world, more of us are getting mad, and we're getting mad more of the time. There is more bullying and anger between teens. More child abuse. More spousal abuse. More office rage. More road rage. There are obvious reasons for this.

Stress levels are on the rise. The future is more uncertain. A nationwide Harris poll in 2002 showed that almost half of all Americans say the tension they feel has worsened over the past year, and more than three-quarters say it is "challenging" to manage stress. Nearly half have come to believe that feeling stressed or tense is "normal."

Life is also speeding up. There's so much to keep up with. As life speeds up, so do your emotional reactions. If you tend to get angry, then you get angry quicker. The same poll showed that fully 81 percent of Americans say they are more impatient with people, and 41 percent admit that their typical behavior when stressed is to be short-tempered and irritable with others. Being irritable and stressed can make you sick. Stress can lead to headaches, irregular heartbeat, or tension in the back, chest, or jaw. When you don't feel well, you can become even more irritable.

The American Institute of Stress estimates that between 75 and 90 percent of doctor visits are for stress-related ailments. Research suggests that psychological distress, including anger, anxiety, and depression, may be good predictors of high blood pressure, and it's estimated that one in four adults in the U.S. now have high blood pressure (American Heart Association 2001). Countless studies link heart disease and sudden cardiac arrest to irritability and anger, hostility and aggressiveness, and nervousness, anxiety, and depression. These studies suggest that accumulated stress from these chronic negative emotions and attitudes is responsible for a substantial percentage of heart attacks and sudden deaths.

The American Academy of Pediatrics estimated in 2000 that one in five children in the U.S. had psychosocial problems related to stress, up from one in fourteen in 1979 (Kelleher et al. 2000). High-strung, angry children are increasingly labeled with attention deficit/hyperactivity disorder, and a growing number of children are now given psychotropic drugs such as Ritalin to help them calm down, focus, and behave in school.

The Environment of Anger

If the stresses of modern life aren't enough to make us angrier, then take a look at the environment of anger we live in. When you think about why you might be angrier, it's important to remember that a lot of anger is being felt and expressed all over the globe. It's communicated incessantly through the media: TV, movies, video games, music, magazines, and the Internet. This builds an environment of anger, making some people quicker to react than they might have been. People unconsciously tune to each other's moods in a kind of emotional telepathy, on a cultural level and in homes, workplaces, and schools.

Here's an example of how emotional telepathy works. You don't want to go to a relative's house for dinner anymore because the family is always yelling and arguing and you always get drawn right into it. You can't resist. You don't find yourself particularly quick to anger in other homes or situations, but you get angry easily there because the negative environment is so strong. Negative environments act like electromagnetic fields. They exert a pull on whomever enters them. Walking into a negative environment, you are more likely to get sucked into angry reactions, dig in your heels, and become irritable and stubborn.

Here's another example of emotional telepathy. Two people at work are talking, and one says something like, "Did you go in that room?" The other answers, "No, I stepped in and turned right around. The anger vibe was so thick you could cut it with a knife." What they're saying is there was such a strong negative energy in the room they feared being swept up in it.

If you find that you're quicker to anger these days, it's helpful to remember that you are not the only one. More people are angry due to the environment of anger surrounding them. The more anger in the world, the more prone people are to get drawn into the magnetic pull of its reactivity. Learning to identify the emotional environment you are exposing yourself to is important in transforming anger. Try to identify where your anger buttons get pushed more easily because of increased stress and negativity in the environment. Many situations are emotional minefields. One person gripes about someone else at work, and pretty soon others are vacuumed in. Or at home, Dad gets angry, so do the kids, and then so does Mom.

Living in a worldwide environment of anger does not release us from the responsibility to manage our emotions. It just helps us understand why managing anger can be harder than it used to be. We still need to do what we can to minimize our contribution to the anger environment. Psychologists urge people to turn off the TV and not keep watching replays of horrific news, lest they continually refuel their anger and anxiety. Yet many people, even those whose intuition tells them to stop watching, cannot tear themselves away and they stay angry and depressed.

So in transforming anger, the first thing to consider is that you are not alone. The next thing to consider is whether you have been taking on other people's anger as your own. How often do you get swept into anger? How often do you add to an environment of anger? A lot of anger is based on a perception of something being unfair, of being wronged, misunderstood, or unable to get what you want or need. When one person starts on this track, others are sure to chime in. Soon everyone is feeling frustrated, fearing their needs won't be met, and blaming others.

The Anger Habit

Another reason we're so mad is because we've gotten mad so often. We've built a pattern of anger in our brains, and when we're on edge any little thing can trigger the anger pattern. Unmet expectations, feeling that you're being treated unfairly, threats to your security or the security of your loved ones or those you care about, threats to your beliefs, threats to your self-image, fearing that the worst will happen—all are common anger triggers. These get amplified the more you react with anger. You tend to see people and life as unfair or out to get you. One distorted perspective leads to another and another until you get madder and madder. Some people get so riled up that they'll scream at a traffic light or a fax machine, blaming an object for delaying them. If you don't take steps to manage your angry reactions, anger is likely to become a strong habit for you.

When you have a long history with anger, when you've put a lot of emotional energy into that anger, you've imprinted a pattern in your brain that's hard to break. For example, say you were neglected or abused as a child. You were wronged, so why shouldn't you be angry forever? After all, if other people are to blame for your anger, then letting go of your anger won't change the wrong done. When anger feels justified, it's easy to keep adding to it.

Resentment is a common emotion that sustains the anger habit. Resentment is a feeling of unhappiness over being wronged or hurt. While what happened might have made anyone upset, if you don't do something to get over it, resentment will fester inside. When people or groups have long-term resentment, they continually give away their power to the person or thing that they resent, without taking responsibility for their thoughts, feelings, and actions. Just consider how often you replay the same hurt and blame over and over again in your mind and words. When the brain is used to reacting in a certain way, it comes to *believe* in its reactions. Resentment is just one example of an *emotional belief*, an ingrained perception from the past that you strongly believe is correct. Emotional beliefs may have come from your own past experience or been handed down from parents, friends, or society. They are built into your neural architecture by your strong emotional investment in them.

Even after your mind knows that resentment is a trap that keeps hurting you and those you care about, knows that you need to let the anger go to move on, your stored emotional beliefs won't let go. They control you. None of this is bad. It's only human. But these stored emotional beliefs can limit how you perceive and respond to situations that anger you.

When trapped in emotional beliefs, you view situations through a narrow-angle lens. Intellectually you know there may be a bigger picture, but emotionally you don't buy it. It's like you have two people living inside you—a rational person ready to move forward, and an emotional person who feels and acts like a hurt child. And emotion calls the shots. When you hear that a coworker talked about you behind your back, how are you likely to react? Not with rational thinking about her troubles or about whether what you heard is even true, but with all the justified anger and resentment that you've been storing up for years. Why? *Because emotions work faster than thoughts.* Your emotional self is suited up and ready for battle before your mental self has an opportunity to consider that maybe anger isn't what's needed in this situation. But you're so used to feeling victimized and angry. Emotional beliefs jump into gear before your mind even has a chance to remember the anger control strategies you've learned. You can get so locked into a habit of anger that you can't see any other choice.

To overcome the habit of anger, you have to identify why you are so mad. What are your sources of anger and your underlying emotional beliefs? Answering the following questions will get you started. Write the questions and your answers on a plain piece of paper or in a notebook. You'll want to keep a *Transforming Anger* journal to keep track of and appreciate your progress as you proceed through this book.

- *Identify ways anger is evident in your home or work environment. How does it affect you?*

- *Are there situations (for example, watching TV news or talk shows, or spending time with negative friends or coworkers) where your anger buttons get pushed more easily because of increased stress and negativity in the environment?*

- *Which of the following are your strongest anger triggers: unmet expectations, feeling that you're being treated unfairly, threats to your security or the security of your loved ones or those you care about, threats to your beliefs, threats to your self-image, fearing that the worst will happen?*

- *What emotional beliefs might be underlying your anger reactions?*

- *What emotional beliefs might be underlying other people's anger reactions?*

- *Think about a person, place, or issue that creates the greatest feelings of anger or resentment in you. What about that person or situation gets you angry most? What is your emotional belief behind that anger?*

Expressions of Anger

People deal with their frustration, anger, and resentment in two main ways: repressing or venting. If you are used to venting, you may yell, swear, hit something, smash objects, or pound pillows. If you are used to repressing anger, you stuff angry feelings down, don't say anything, and blame yourself. Some people use both ways and can be passive-aggressive. But neither venting nor repressing transforms the anger. It's still there seething inside.

If you're someone who vents, you may think anger feels good because of the sense of justification and the rush of adrenaline and release it gives you, but this is only temporary. When you come down from an anger high, you're often more drained and cranky than before your outburst. You may also have to deal with consequences of your anger—smashed objects, other people's feelings, the law—which can drain you even more. People who vent do let off steam, but venting only keeps reinforcing the habit of anger.

If you're someone who represses anger, you have a fire going on in your body all the time. The fire takes energy to keep burning, and after a while it causes exhaustion, headaches, stomachaches, heart problems, or other illnesses. If you are passive-aggressive, you become sullen or use your anger to intimidate or force others into giving you what you want.

chapter 3

What's the Heart Got to Do with It?

Now that you've identified some of the sources of your anger and looked at how you express your anger, you're ready to gain an understanding of the most reliable, powerful ally that you can ever have to transform your anger. It's your heart. That might sound like a metaphor you've heard before — one that's too sweet and simple to be very useful. But now there's scientific understanding of how the power of the heart can change your brain and body and transform an anger habit. The mind and emotions can be brought into coherence, but it takes the heart to do that. It's important to understand how this works.

Joyce identifies work pressures and constant interruptions as the main things that get her angry. She feels tense most of the time and has frequent headaches. Joyce says,

> *I have to multitask, answer e-mails, make phone calls, and get reports done at high speed. When someone interrupts me and breaks my focus, I feel like punching them in the face. After I get home, the multitasking goes on. My kids and husband are always interrupting me. I can feel my heart race and my face get flushed. One night the phone rang while*

> *I was yelling at my fifteen-year-old to stop picking on his sister and trying to keep dinner from burning on the stove at the same time. When I finally got to the phone, it was some telemarketing jerk and I threw the phone across the room.*

Does Joyce's experience sound like your own? The amount of multitasking many of us do can exacerbate a short fuse. Ongoing irritation or frustration can cause chronic imbalances in your nervous system and hormonal and immune systems, which keep you on edge. Why? Because continuing negative reactions keep your heart, brain, and body out of sync. Joyce discovered how to transform her anger so she was able to handle multitasking without letting it drain her. First, she learned what her anger reactions were doing to her body.

What Happens in Your Body When You Feel Anger?

In the past decade, researchers have discovered that the heart is a major player in the emotional system. The heart is an information-processing system. There are actually more nerves going from heart to brain than from brain to heart (McCraty forthcoming). The heart communicates information to the brain and the rest of the body via four different kinds of pathways: *neurological* (nervous system), *biochemical* (hormones and neurotransmitters), *biophysical* (blood pressure waves), and *energetic* (electromagnetic fields). All of this information originates *within* the heart itself.

Your heart's beat-to-beat rhythmic pattern, called *heart rate variability* or HRV, is very sensitive to your changing emotional states. Scientists and health professionals now use HRV analysis as an important measure of many things, including a person's degree of mental and emotional stress.

HRV has been found to be an accurate indicator of nervous system aging rate (Umetani et al. 1998) and even a predictor of mortality from all diseases (Tsuji et al. 1994).

The HRV pattern has a disordered and chaotic rhythm when you experience stressful emotions such as anger, irritation, or frustration. This is called an *incoherent* HRV pattern (see figure 1). Displayed on a computer screen, an incoherent heart rhythm pattern looks rough and jagged—just like you feel inside. By contrast, when you feel positive emotions such as love, care, or appreciation, your heart rhythm pattern becomes more ordered. This is called a *coherent* pattern. Positive emotions create a smooth, coherent, sine-wave-like pattern, and you feel more coherent inside. Your brain functions more efficiently and you think more clearly (Tiller, McCraty, and Atkinson 1996).

A coherent heart rhythm pattern also indicates a state of balance and synchronization between the two branches of your *autonomic nervous system,* the part of your nervous system that controls involuntary processes like heart rate, digestion, and hormonal control. The *sympathetic* branch speeds up your heart rate, and the *parasympathetic* branch slows it down. Positive emotions and coherent heart rhythms cause the parasympathetic and sympathetic nervous systems to operate in harmony. They create a state we call *emotional coherence.* Negative emotions cause these two parts of the

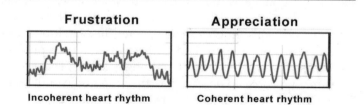

Frustration

Incoherent heart rhythm

Appreciation

Coherent heart rhythm

Figure 1

autonomic nervous system to get out of sync (McCraty et al. 1995). This creates emotional incoherence.

Feeling irritated, frustrated, angry, and emotionally incoherent much of the time puts your sympathetic nervous system into overdrive. When you're under this kind of stress, it's like driving a car with one foot on the gas pedal (the sympathetic nervous system) and the other foot on the brake (parasympathetic nervous system) at the same time. It creates a jerky ride—at best—and you burn a lot more gas. Just as this causes extra wear and tear on the car, emotional incoherence causes extra stress on your nervous system and body. It depletes your energy and interferes with your ability to think.

Other factors, like getting addicted to the adrenaline rush of constant stimulation, also create an overactive sympathetic system. Chronic activation of the sympathetic nervous system makes it harder to get calm or slow down when you need to. This increases the risk of cardiac arrhythmias and sudden cardiac death. Reports showed a sixfold increase in life-threatening cardiac arrhythmias in the hours, days, and weeks after the terrorist attacks of September 11, 2001 (Steinberg et al. 2002). This is most likely explained by a significant reduction in the calming protection normally offered by the parasympathetic nervous system (Lampert et al. 2002).

When persistent emotional incoherence keeps your sympathetic nervous system in overdrive, it can lead to nervous system exhaustion. It can also cause hormonal imbalances, such as a chronic elevation in the "stress hormone," cortisol, and a reduction in dehydroepiandrosterone (DHEA), the "vitality" or "anti-aging" hormone. Over time, a chronic elevation of cortisol resets the body's thermostat to keep producing cortisol even when you're no longer angry. That's why when many people go on vacation, they can't relax or it takes them days to unwind. That's also why many people can't sleep well at night. Too much cortisol over too long a time period also triggers excessive fat build up (especially around the waist and hips), impairs immune function, decreases bone and muscle mass, impairs memory and learning, and destroys brain cells (McCraty, Barrios-Choplin, et al. 1998).

In today's fast-paced life, one of the factors contributing to high stress (and high cortisol production) is that life moves too fast for emotions to keep up. This puts extra strain on the heart and nervous system. Like Joyce, many people have work and family demands that require them to shift focus many, many times an hour. Each time you react to a demand or an interruption with irritation or frustration, it's like squirting more cortisol into your body. Each pinprick of irritation drains your emotional energy, and you get exhausted. No wonder so many people have stress-related illnesses and are more prone to resentment.

A Fast Track for Turning Around Negatives

Because the heart is a primary generator of rhythm in the body—influencing brain processes that control your nervous system, your emotions, and your cognitive functions—the heart provides an access point from which these system-wide dynamics can be quickly and profoundly affected.

When you shift your heart rhythms into more coherence, you also shift your emotions into more coherence, and bring your autonomic nervous system into balance. By learning to shift your heart rhythms *right when you feel frustration or anger,* you harness the physiological power of anger. You take back the power you already own inside. You change the information going from your heart to your brain. You facilitate your higher brain functions and think more coherently.

Thousands of self-help books and philosophies talk about turning around your negative reactions and thoughts through relaxation, breathing, affirmations, or cognitive techniques. What's missing? You need heart rhythm coherence to have enough power to really shift emotion and see a bigger picture.

Because the heart impacts the rest of the body so strongly, all you have to do to stop your stress is to shift your heart rhythms away from the incoherent, jagged pattern and toward the ordered, coherent pattern. Doing this is simple: you *choose the heart* by shifting your focus of attention to your heart and breathing through that area of your body. Try this now. As you breathe, genuinely hold a positive attitude like care or appreciation, and breathe that attitude through your heart. It can take a little practice to do this. As you practice, *your feeling and perception change.* You escape from old emotional patterns. Controlling your heart rhythm pattern will give you more control over your autonomic nervous system, a part of the body that scientists always thought was beyond conscious control unless you were a saint or yoga master.

Wide-Angle Lens or Narrow Focus?

Learning to connect with your heart changes your life. You gain access to a source of wisdom and power that you probably have tapped into only now and then. Think back to a time, maybe when you were taking a shower, walking outdoors, or feeling relaxed, when you had an "aha!" experience. You got an answer and intuitively knew it was right—and it was! You felt great, like anything was possible. Or think of a time when you were newly in love, or you'd just been appreciated for a job well done, or you were serenely enjoying a sunset in the tropics with the wind caressing your hair. In these moments, you felt expansive and secure. Your heart rhythms were in sync, and correspondingly your perception was relaxed and open, like a wide-angle lens that's able to see everything.

By contrast, when you're feeling stressed and mad and your heart rhythms are disordered and incoherent, your focus narrows, like a camera lens zooming in on only one thing. Why does this happen? Because your heart's incoherent rhythms are inhibiting your higher brain functions. Furthermore, your sympathetic nervous system is triggering the release of adrenaline, putting your body in survival mode. In survival mode, you *can't* think as coherently. You don't need to. Facing a snarling dog, you don't need to carefully consider the pros and cons of the situation! All you need to do is run or defend yourself. Stress narrows your lens of perception to the threat at hand. A narrow focus is helpful when you're in danger, but it's not helpful if you're trying to understand a complex or sensitive situation and make the most effective choice possible.

The physiological response of anger is designed to protect your body's vital functions and to prepare you to strike out or run away from whatever might threaten your security. It doesn't matter whether the threat is external (like an attack by an animal) or internal (like fearing something is out to get you). You feel trapped, and you are. You can see no way out.

What's worse, anger makes you *believe* that you're seeing things accurately even when you're not. Frustration becomes a way of living. You develop a short fuse based on constant conflict between your expectations of how life should be and the reality of how life seems to be. Resentment builds. You feel victimized. If others would just change even a little bit, then everything would be okay. This is how you develop an anger habit. But it doesn't make you happy. Anger never does. It can't.

Learning how to smooth out your heart rhythm pattern widens the aperture of your lens of perception so you can see more options. A smooth, coherent heart rhythm helps calm your nerves and lowers blood pressure (McCraty et al. 1995). It improves immunity and creates more balanced hormonal production (Rein, Atkinson, and McCraty 1995). It also changes the electromagnetic field that radiates from your heart to your entire body, to other people, and to the world around you. The pattern of your heart rhythm is broadcast through that field and literally can change others' hearts (McCraty in press).

Heart rhythm coherence helps normalize the energies within you. It helps clear the slate of ineffective emotional beliefs so you can act from your higher self. You intuitively know what's best for the whole situation—but you know through the heart. Coherence also helps you protect yourself from other people's negativity by offsetting the pull of the electromagnetic field around you.

Try the "Choosing the Heart" exercise and "Attitude Breathing" tool to get a feel for the power of coherence.

✎ Choosing the Heart

Can you remember a personal or professional situation where you chose to act from the heart — in other words, where you felt balanced and responded to another individual with more understanding, care, or appreciation than you normally would have? Remember the feeling it gave you. What was the other person's response? What was the outcome — short- and long-term — of that choice? Write down your answers for future reference.

Now remember a time when you didn't act from your heart, and consider how that situation turned out. Note the difference in how you felt. That's the difference between coherence and incoherence.

✎ Attitude Breathing Tool

Attitude Breathing is a simple tool. Use it whenever you feel irritated, frustrated, angry, anxious, or any time you need more coherence. Attitude Breathing can take the "fire" out of negative thoughts and emotions so they have less fuel and power.

Attitude Breathing requires that you plan ahead by choosing a positive emotion to draw on, like love, appreciation, care, compassion, or balance. Take a moment to remember the feeling you identified in the previous exercise, when you chose to follow your heart. This is the feeling of emotional coherence you are striving for. Don't worry if you can't find a positive feeling or if you have inner resistance. Just trying to sincerely shift to a positive attitude of appreciation, compassion, or care will increase your coherence. You can always find a genuine attitude of care even when you feel resistance inside or can't find a feeling of care.

1. *For most people, appreciation is the easiest positive emotion to shift to in the heat of the moment, so we'll focus on appreciation. To prepare to use this tool, take a moment to build an attitude of appreciation for someone or something in your life. Imagine you are breathing that feeling of appreciation through your heart for two or three breaths.*

2. *Now focus on your heart and solar plexus (abdominal area) together, and keep breathing appreciation through that area. Ask yourself, "What would be a better attitude for me to maintain in this situation?" Then set up an inner attitude like "stay calm," "stay neutral in this situation," "don't judge before you know the facts," "make peace with this," "have more compassion," or whatever attitude you decide is appropriate.*

3. *Next, gently and sincerely pretend to breathe the new attitude in through the heart. Then breathe it out through the solar plexus and stomach to anchor it in your body. Do this for a while until you feel the new attitude has set in.*

Attitude Breathing is a useful tool in a wide variety of situations. When Joyce learned Attitude Breathing and started using it at work, she became more aware of her tendencies to blame other people when she got interrupted or when something went wrong, and to get angry about issues or decisions that felt unfair. She also noticed that everybody else was doing the same thing. "When I started shifting my attitude with the heart breathing," says Joyce, "I quickly could see creative solutions that I just couldn't before." Joyce had discovered the power of the wider lens. "At times, I couldn't believe how smoothly things went or how easy it was to get what I wanted done, whereas before I had felt blocked by people and circumstances."

Continue to practice Choosing the Heart and Attitude Breathing as you're reading this book. If negative emotional associations get triggered while you're reading, practice one of these tools to help you find a heart perception, and new insights will begin to unfold.

Here are other important times to use Attitude Breathing:

When you wake up in the morning. Negative thoughts and emotions like worry, sadness, hurt, or anger can often creep in as soon as you wake up in the morning, sometimes before you even get out of bed. That's where the expression "getting up on the wrong side of the bed" comes from!

Practice Attitude Breathing for the first thirty minutes or hour after you awaken, during your preparations for the day. You can do it while showering, getting dressed, or commuting to work. Those negative thoughts and attitudes you wake up with can quickly increase in momentum if you don't neutralize them and replace them with attitudes that are not draining and self-defeating. Choose thoughts and attitudes—like appreciation or care—that would benefit your day, and breathe them in through the heart and out through the solar plexus and abdomen for a few moments to increase coherence. The outward breath through the solar plexus anchors the attitude.

If you start your morning with stress-producing attitudes or frustrations, they gain strength quickly, setting up a continuous emotional loop that's hard to shake off. Negative morning thoughts and emotions, if left unchecked, can create a pressing momentum that can sap your vitality even before noon. This can leave you feeling apathetic, unproductive, and quick to anger for the rest of the day.

If you find any of those negative morning thoughts or emotions returning during your day, take a moment to refocus on a positive replacement attitude and begin to practice Attitude Breathing again for a little while. Remember that you don't have to stop regular activities to use the Attitude Breathing tool.

When you're feeling tense. A buildup of tension is an indicator of being out of balance emotionally. Some of us accumulate tension in the area of the chest. We may experience shortness of breath, heart palpitations, or irregular heartbeat. Others experience tension as a headache or a knot in the stomach, back, neck, or shoulders. Use Attitude Breathing to help release tension in any part of the body. As you do this, ask yourself, "What would be a more balanced feeling or approach to what I'm doing?" Once you feel more emotionally balanced, pretend to breathe the feeling of balance through the area of tension. You'll start to feel the tension release as more of your coherent heart energy moves through that area.

When you want to stop emotional reactivity. During stressful times, it helps to realize that many people are experiencing negative emotions, such as uncertainty, frustration, fear, anger, and rage. This can make everyone around you edgy and irritable. It's especially important to have compassion for yourself and others during times that are challenging for everyone. As soon as you catch yourself getting irritated, frustrated, angry, or enraged, use Attitude Breathing to take the excess negative emotion out of your reaction and to shift into heart rhythm coherence. Anchoring your energy in your heart and solar plexus will help you stay centered and see calmly and clearly how best to respond.

Transforming the Anger Habit

To transform a habit of anger that has been reinforced by your emotional beliefs and neural patterns, you have to harness the power of your physiology. You have to transform the physiology of anger into the more powerful physiology of love. You do this by connecting with the power of your heart. As you learn techniques to get your heart rhythms into more coherence and breathe love, appreciation, or care, you stop old mechanical emotional reactions—quick, reflexive responses that come from your head, not your real heart. You generate physiological changes that expand your perceptions. As you gain a wider perspective, you become able to move out of neural patterns that keep reigniting your anger. You generate a more coherent electromagnetic field that you and others can draw healing and sustenance from. This adds more power to your efforts to reorganize your reactions and responses, and to reorganize your life.

Heart rhythm coherence gives us all the power to get past old emotional beliefs and habits. Choosing the heart means choosing a new way of looking at things—a broader, more flexible way of viewing the world and ourselves. Choosing the heart means choosing attitudes of love, care, and appreciation—for ourselves and others.

> *feeling of anxiety came up, then an image of my*
> *friend looking at me coldly. I immediately thought of*
> *a time we had a fight and the hurt feeling I had. I*
> *was sure he was going to say something at lunch*
> *today that would be hurtful. For the next mile I was*
> *brooding with anger. Then I stopped myself. I started*
> *laughing when I realized there was nothing wrong*
> *and I was just assuming all this. We actually had a*
> *great lunch.*

Emotional projections keep you looking at the future through the same lens you've used to look at past incidents. Emotional projections don't give you or the other person a chance to act differently. Emotional projections are one of the most potent anger triggers. Think back to a time you got angry because you assumed someone was going to be "that way" again the next time you saw him or her. Psychologists often describe how a memory leads to an interpretation, then to a projection, then to an assumption, and then—boom!— you're angry. This process triggers a rapid-fire sequence of feelings, images, and thoughts that we call the *anger cascade*.

The key to stopping the anger cascade is paying attention to the *feeling* that comes up with the memory. Karla first noticed a feeling of anxiety. When she wondered what that was about, she recalled a memory of her friend looking hostile, then the interpretation followed. Very often feelings come first, before thoughts. If you can catch the feeling and discover the memory that triggered it, you are well on the way to stopping the flow of thoughts and interpretations that lead to the anger cascade. Nothing was happening in the car that warranted Karla's anger. It was all triggered by an emotional memory inspired by the initial feeling of anxiety.

What goes on in your neural circuits during this anger cascade has everything to do with how you perceive and feel. A memory can trigger a perception, which triggers feelings and thoughts, which trigger physiological changes in your heart, brain, nervous, and hormonal systems. Repetition of this cascade imprints the pattern in your neural circuitry. Once imprinted, it becomes an *emotional belief.* Your brain is used to believing things are a certain way and triggers the same set of emotional and physiological responses. However, if you can shift your emotions or your perception at any point in the cascade, you'll launch a different set of thoughts, feelings, and physiological effects. By using the HeartMath tools to shift emotion and perception, you can begin the process of rewiring your brain and repatterning your nervous system. You can learn to recognize and stop the anger triggers, then choose to go down a different path, one with new thoughts and feelings.

If you look at the triggers that get you the angriest, you can see how often a memory or a projection fuels your anger. This is important because memories tend to distort your perception of current events and views of the future. Emotional projections drain a lot of emotional and nervous system energy, and that drain also stops you from seeing clearly.

Most people, in their calmer moments, know that certain emotional projections might not be accurate. Or people like Karla, who aren't often angry, can catch an emotional projection while it's happening and stop it. Once emotional projections and your angry reactions to them get started, your intelligence is hijacked. You're no longer able to be open to what's happening in the present; you just assume what you're emotionally believing is true. You see things exaggerated or in extremes instead of in balance. The end result is that you feel helpless and out of control.

Common Anger Projections

See if you recognize any of the following common emotional projections, rationalizations, and assumptions in yourself.

All-or-nothing thinking. "She turned me down for a date. No one wants to go out with me." "Look at the mistake she made. She must be a total loser." "He didn't return my stapler. He doesn't give a damn about anyone except himself." "He's always selfish." "She's always stupid and thoughtless." All-or-nothing thinking triggers anger because it makes you feel helpless. You can't see any other options, so you lash out like a cornered animal.

Blaming and accusing. "That driver in front of me is deliberately going too slowly. I'll show him." "The boss criticized my handwriting. He's out to get me. I'm sure I'll be fired." "It's all his fault that my life turned out this way." "People always ignore my needs." "People always demand or expect too much from me, take advantage of me, use me, control me, shame or criticize me, keep me waiting, manipulate me, disrespect me," and so on. Blame comes from emotional projections that something or someone has been unfair, which we then use to rationalize feeling angry. Blame is a common trigger for anger. Just think about the last time you blamed someone else for something that had gone wrong. Did anger automatically follow?

Judging. "He has no taste." "She's a real witch." "He's going to be 'that way' again." "I'm a terrible mother." The list of put-downs can go on and on and on inside your mind and emotional world. Behind every emotional projection and assumption that leads to all-or-nothing thinking, blaming, and accusing, you'll find a judgment. Some judgments, like the ones listed above, are obvious. You speak the words in your head or aloud. Other judgments are so automatic and matter-of-fact that you don't notice them. Or you don't believe you are judging because "it's just the way things are." Yet those entrenched judgments trigger your anger and rule your life. Here's an example of how judgments stop the progress of two people trying to work out their differences.

Two people had an argument and decided to talk and sort things out. After they'd finished, one said, "I'm okay, are you okay?" The other said, "Yeah, I'm fine." They went their separate ways. "He's such a jerk," thought one. "Glad that's over, but I won't talk to her again," thought the other. They both let these judgmental thoughts cascade into seething anger without the other knowing it. Judgments are emotional projections based on "just knowing something." They limit you and the person you are judging.

Neutralizing a Projection

To stop the anger cascade, you need to pay attention to the feeling or memory that triggers judgmental or angry thoughts. You need to neutralize that emotional projection as soon as it happens. Going to Neutral stops the energy drain in your system and gives you a chance to see more options. A lot of times, people judge others based on rumors they've heard. Have you ever seen friends or coworkers get mad over a rumor that later proved false or only partially true? Think about how often you've done this. Or think about how often you've found that situations weren't nearly as bad as you had judged them to be—after you had already wasted loads of energy and drained yourself. Remembering these experiences can give you practical reasons to learn a tool like Go to Neutral, which we'll explain later in this chapter. Learning to neutralize a projection can save much inner turmoil and help you avoid health problems.

Let's say you overheard someone at work mentioning your name, but she didn't know you heard her. She was saying something about you that you couldn't totally make out, but you guessed by the laughter that it was disrespectful and you felt hurt. The hurt lasted a while, and then you started getting mad. An hour later you were stewing and finally you were frying. (It sounds like you were preparing a chicken dinner!) You stewed all evening and, of course, seethed all night because it would be tomorrow before you could give her a piece of your mind.

The next day, you decided to listen to your heart intuition suggesting that you check out your assumption first. You asked one of the people who was present whether your coworker said anything about you. He laughed and said, "Yes, she was admiring how you stood up to that copier repair man who was trying to give you the runaround." You breathed a sigh of relief and felt *so* glad that you checked things out.

But what about the energy that got wasted while you were stewing and frying for twenty-four hours? How many times have you emotionally drained yourself and found out later that it was all for nothing? Consider the flood of stress hormones you could have avoided if you had been able to stay in a neutral place until you had all the facts. Stewing, seething, frying, boiling—these are all words to indicate strong emotions that can flood your bloodstream with stress hormones if you don't find a way to let go of them. These hormones suppress the immune system, setting you up for emotional and physical health problems.

Negative judgments are what keep assumptions alive and stress hormones flowing. Often people think they don't judge because they don't say anything out loud. However, judgments take place at the feeling level. Negative judgmental feelings, especially when constantly replayed internally, sap your vitality. To understand the negative side of judgment, it helps to remember how it feels when you are judged, especially if it's for something you didn't do or say. Realize that many of your judgments are about people you are close to and often forgive anyway—*later*. It helps to forgive and let go, but most people don't consider the amount of stress hormones they've produced before they decide to let go of something. This is where finding a neutral place in the heart really can help, by keeping your reaction energy at a minimum until you can forgive and let go of the anger.

The Go to Neutral tool will help keep you from jumping headlong into memories, judgments, projections, and assumptions that cascade into anger. Using Go to Neutral will help you move away from these thought and feeling patterns and reestablish balance. Go to Neutral allows you to step back from your racing mind and your emotionally charged feelings. This gives you a chance to pause your emotions and thoughts long enough to consider the consequences and options: Do you want to increase those negative feelings that produce stress hormones and drain your system? Or would you like to prevent that stress by chilling out in neutral until your emotions cool down, then be able to see more clearly and do what's best? Can you remember the last time you let the anger cascade run its course and how miserable you felt? Do you really want to cut yourself off from the person you're angry with and maybe later regret it?

You can find neutral fast by engaging the power of the heart. Here's how you do it.

✐ Go to Neutral Tool

1. *Take a time-out so that you can temporarily disengage from your thoughts and feelings, especially stressful ones. When emotional triggers come up, recognize that you are triggering. As soon as you feel the trigger, tell yourself "time-out!" and step back from the reaction.*

2. *Shift your focus to the area around your heart. Now feel your breath coming in through your heart and going out through your solar plexus. Practice breathing this way a few times to ease into a time-out in the heart.*

3. *Tell yourself, "Go to Neutral," then don't go one way or the other in your thoughts or feelings about the issue. Hold onto a*

> *place of being neutral in the heart until your emotions ease up and your perception relaxes.*

Pick an emotionally charged situation and try this tool right now. Just recalling the situation might bring up some of the emotions associated with it. Use Go to Neutral as those emotions arise and see if you can't begin to neutralize and ease some of your reactions. If you start to slide back down the anger cascade, restart — use the steps of Go to Neutral again. At first you may have to practice Go to Neutral a dozen times or more before you have enough heart power to hang in neutral. That's fine. It's like building a muscle, and it takes exercise. To gain more heart power to stay in neutral, add the Attitude Breathing tool from chapter 3 and breathe appreciation for your efforts and for any progress. If you can't find an appreciative attitude, then just breathe an attitude of compassion or an attitude of neutral through your heart and solar plexus to help anchor it into your system.

If you were able to find a neutral attitude about the emotionally charged situation you picked to practice on, or at least got there partway, you may have some different thoughts now about the situation. If you continue to use Go to Neutral about it more often, how do you think your life might be different? Write down any new thoughts, feelings, or insights in your notebook to help remind you. Describe what Go to Neutral felt like in your own words.

Neutral is a place where you have more options. In neutral, you don't have to buy into an old memory, a projection, or an assumption. You get to a point where you can honestly admit you don't know all the whys or wherefores and thus you can choose not to react. Once in neutral, you have the space to ask yourself questions like, "What if it's not like I'm thinking it is?" "What if there's something I don't know?" "What if I really don't know?" Just asking your heart "What if. . . ?" from a neutral point opens the gate for new intelligence to come to you — or for insights you've already had to become available to you again. The attitude of

"I don't know" helps the mind become humble and surrender to the heart so that intuitive heart intelligence can surface.

When you Go to Neutral, you harness your emotional power. Neutral depersonalizes the issue so you don't go overboard one way or another. It builds patience and allows for more possibilities to emerge. Neutral is a place within you where your wise self can talk to your disturbed self and save you a lot of headache and emotional strife — if you'll listen.

Going to Neutral in the heart will take practice. Why? Because usually we try to become neutral in our *thoughts* before we've learned to neutralize our *feelings*. People tell each other "Just stay neutral," "I'm neutral about it, are you neutral?" You can say yes, but neutral from the mind doesn't last long unless your emotions and heart are also put in neutral.

Emotionally charged feelings can be hard to shift on the spot. Sometimes you are only able to go halfway. At these times, neutral involves temporarily making peace with what isn't peaceful. In other words, you Go to Neutral about still feeling disturbed, and that will neutralize and eliminate some of the disturbance.

The Heart Feels Different

Your heart is always communicating its state to the brain and the rest of the body. The heart communicates through neurological, hormonal, vascular, and electromagnetic pathways. The heart helps guide the entire system towards increased order, awareness, and coherence. That's why you have more intelligence when you learn to listen to your heart. Your heart intelligence takes the form of intuitions or perceptions that *feel* different from projections, judgmental feelings, or assumptions. You'll learn how to recognize the difference in yourself.

Kay used to be confused about what were her intuitive feelings and how they were different from judgmental feelings. "I finally realized that my intuitive feelings are accompanied by a sense of peace or ease or at least neutral. My judgmental feelings are followed by a negative reaction of irritation, hurt, or anger. I find this very interesting." Kay explains,

> I was having one of those days, when my husband called me at work about something or other. I don't even remember the issue, just the feeling. I felt my anger arise and got very quiet on the phone. I knew if I said anything at that very moment based on what I was thinking, I'd regret it later. I hung up the phone and needed to get back to work, but I couldn't. I was too angry. I took a deep breath and decided to take a few minutes to calm down, Go to Neutral in my heart, and find something to appreciate to get into some coherence. I remembered what it is about my husband I appreciate. I made a mental list and started to feel — not just think about — all the appreciation I have for him and our life together. I felt better and got back to work.
>
> When I got home my husband asked, "So how long did you fume over our conversation?" With a smile on my face I replied, "Oh, about five seconds. I just remembered what it is about you I appreciate, and I didn't feel angry anymore!" Surprised, he wanted to know what that list was! We had a great evening.

The Courage to Listen to Your Heart

It takes courage to listen to your heart intuition, because often what it will tell you can seem too soft, simple, or easy. Your heart intuition might say, "Just let it go" or "It's no big deal," and you'll be afraid that you're going to let someone get away with something or that the other person is going to walk all over you. It takes strength to follow what your heart says, to see whether its advice turns out to be effective or not. It's in that in-between moment, when your heart rhythm is more coherent, your system more in sync, when you have a window of opportunity to listen and do what your heart intuition says, and to go against the grain of insecurities and emotional projections.

Life gets more interesting as you learn to look at your anger triggers from your heart's perspective. You'll be better prepared to recognize emotional triggers and stop the bullets. You'll also have more power to stop thoughts that replay in your head and refuel your anger. Remember to be sincere and genuine in practicing Go to Neutral, so that you're shifting your feelings using the strength of your heart, not your mind. Through the power of your heart, you can effectively rearrange your emotions so they don't keep rearranging you!

chapter 5

Knowing Your Head from Your Heart

Learning to choose a heart-intelligent response when you get triggered puts you in charge of your own life. You're no longer at the mercy of strong emotions and old hurts — your own or others'. You retrain your neural circuits so that coherence becomes the norm, which helps widen the aperture of your lens of perception, giving you new insights into yourself and those around you. You understand what Mark Twain meant when he said, "One learns people through the heart, not the eyes or the intellect."

It gets easier to change old responses based on projections, inflexible attitudes, all-or-nothing thinking, and mechanical reactions once you realize *they all come from the same source.* They all come from being stuck "in your head," out of sync with your deeper self. Your deeper self resides in the heart, in the security that flows from centering yourself in feelings of care and appreciation.

You tap into the real you by knowing the difference between being "in the head" and "in the heart." It's like two different radio stations. Tuned to the heart station, your attitude adjusts and you find responses that are much more satisfying to you and better for everyone involved.

The Power to Change

When you *really* want to change, reinforcement will come from your heart. Your heart wants to get out of the anger trap and not have to endure the hurt, resentment, and anguish anymore. Your heart will motivate you to improve your relationship, save your job, or even stay out of jail.

Love is integral to motivation. Feelings of care and appreciation move you out of old hurts and resentments as you realize you don't need to hang on to them to feel secure. Love makes it possible for you to shift to a wide-angle lens of perception. Take Sam, for instance. Sam was constantly annoyed by his parents. Every time he visited them, he felt his anger triggered. Then Sam fell in love. Riding high and feeling great about himself, he saw his parents in a new way. Their reactions no longer bothered him. Instead of making him want to run a hundred miles, their reactions slipped off him like water off a duck's back. Why?

When you're in love, your heart is more open. The hormones released from being in love give you a more cushioned response to situations.

You can build that same cushion from within. You don't need to wait to fall in love. Learning how to generate more love in your own system creates that cushion, so you react to people or events not with an angry survival response but with a *centered* and secure response. The heart tools build security, and inner security is what gives you the power to change.

The heart really is about transformation. That's part of nature's design. Your heart transforms the physiology of anger, which drains your system, into the physiology of love, which gives you wholeness and effectiveness. You achieve this by replacing angry emotions with real care. Feelings of care and appreciation are the building blocks of love.

When you replace anger with care, you choose a more effective emotion. Care transforms perception. Care is an ingredient of intelligence that causes your entire system to work more harmoniously and respond more effectively to resistances that come up in life. Care gives you rhythm. Life happens, stuff happens. Self-generated care enables you to move through setbacks, inner resistances, and inconveniences with more intelligence and less energy. Here's a picture.

You are in a crowded airport and late getting to your plane. You start to push your way anxiously through the crowd, bumping into luggage and people, frustrated because you can't move as fast as you need to. You're angry at whomever is in your way. Your head is driving you. If you take a moment to get centered in your heart and find an attitude of appreciation or care, your flow changes. You see the openings in the throng and feel your way through in a rhythm, dancing around obstacles, getting to your gate with minimum energy expenditure. That's what tuning to your heart rhythm can do.

The heart rhythm is subtle. To find it when you need it requires a new secure reference place inside, from which you respond — a heart-intelligent place. That reference place will feel different from your reactive "head" place, but you'll come to recognize it. So how do you tell the difference?

Distinguishing Your Head from Your Heart

Have you ever stopped to listen to the sound of the head? Below are some typical examples of how the head sounds in someone who's quick to get frustrated or angry.

Driving. "How long is this going to take?" "Damn this traffic!" "Stupid driver, slowing everyone down." "When are they going to widen this road? You pay taxes but nothing happens." "She just cut in deliberately!" (Give her the finger.)

Home. "Why is this place such a mess?" "He just doesn't care!" "I can't stand those kids not picking up." "They don't give a damn about me." "Where's the remote?" "Why didn't someone buy soda?" "Why isn't dinner done?" "Don't look at me like that!" (Blow up.)

Work. "Who does she think she is? It's not fair she gets the good assignments and I'm left with crap—makes me furious!" "He's always sucking up to the boss." "There's no way to keep up—that damn printer keeps jamming!" (Slam the printer tray and break it.)

The supermarket. "Why don't they have more checkout people? They keep us standing here like cattle—they know people are busy." "And the prices you have to pay! They don't give a damn." "That dumb mother can't keep her kid's hands off the candy. Someone should teach the brat a lesson." (Head shaking, blood pressure rising.) "This place is a dump. I'm outta here!" (Slam car door, drive crazily, take frustration out on the dog, kids, spouse—whomever you see or whatever you do next.)

In all these examples, your judgments are in control and you feel justified in being judgmental and angry. Maybe the emotional telepathy has got to you. After all, as you're driving, other angry drivers are reacting and possibly judging you. At work, others are blaming and complaining. At home, other family members are frustrated, possibly with you. Angry people tend to set off the emotional energy of others. The heart is heard only occasionally because it's beneath the din of the head noise. Even if you hear your heart intuition suggesting another response, it's easy to dismiss it and go back to the head. Or you disbelieve the heart's voice as ineffectual. Anger gives more of a rush.

Yielding to the head's noise, you get caught in a downward spiral of blame and anger. But you have the power to escape by becoming more aware of your heart's voice of common sense. *You can start to anchor and empower yourself by using a heart tool like Attitude Breathing or Go to Neutral. Your heart intuition or intelligence will come in louder.*

What will the heart say? The sound of the heart is very different from the head. Here are typical examples of your heart talking.

Driving. "Traffic isn't going to move until it moves—no use getting upset. Turn on the CD player and listen to some music." "That woman is really upset. Send her some heart."

Home. "I really don't like the house messy. We need a better plan for keeping the house in order. Let me arrange a talk with Stan and the kids after dinner. No TV or distractions until we've created a plan. We'll set up consequences if one of us doesn't do what we agreed to and rewards if we do. It could be fun if we do it together."

Work. "Things are tough. Everyone's running fast and trying to just keep their job. I need to keep my cool and not drain my energy, not get into the backbiting, make sure I take my breaks. My intuition says it would be a good idea to sincerely get to know some of these people better, maybe have lunch once in a while."

The supermarket. "I really didn't plan this right. The checker looks like she's been working twelve hours—send her some care. Let me see what magazine on the news rack I can read while I'm waiting."

Quite often you know in your heart what to do—and have strong intentions to do it—but something is missing so you can't follow through. A lot of people talk about "knowing better," but that doesn't help fix things so they can "do better." *The Heart Lock-In technique we'll show you later in this chapter will help you find that missing piece — the new reference place in your heart.* Understanding a little more about the head and how it stores emotions will help you use Heart Lock-In most effectively.

The Mechanism of Emotional Histories

All of the judgments made by the head develop their force through the power of emotional memory. The feelings you had in the past are your *emotional history.* Your emotional history gets stored by the *amygdala* (ah-MIG-dah-la), which is an almond-sized structure in the brain. The amygdala triggers automatic reactions based on your experience of similar things that happened in the past.

A feeling of fear in the present can be triggered by a previous situation that left a strong emotional impression. The more negative emotional investment you have in the past situation, the stronger the fear feeling will be in the present. For example, Don was rejected by a woman he loved. He caught her with another man, and she packed her things and left. Don was deeply hurt, and it took him years to get over the pain and anger. Now, in his new relationship, every time his wife talks to another guy, Don feels fear. The fear gets triggered so fast that the cognitive centers of his brain don't have time to consider if fear is really warranted. He just reacts, gets upset, then gets angry. This is because the amygdala goes for the familiar — it tries to find a match between what's happening now and what happened before. Perceiving a threat or even something that resembles a threat, Don's amygdala triggers a response based on his emotional history. The amygdala then sends a "fear" message to his frontal lobes, which determine the appropriate action. Unless something else overrides the fear, his brain will choose an action based on fear even if it is an irrational response (Pribram 1991).

Remember Karla from chapter 4? As Karla drove to lunch, her emotional history triggered anxiety, then she projected a picture of an old memory, and anger followed. The amygdala stores patterns that get frozen in place by strong emotion. These crystallized patterns exert a strong pull, which keeps you stuck in old responses. Have you ever heard yourself react and sound just like your mother or father? Their emotional patterns created a strong impression in you, so you now respond in the same way.

Here's another example of how emotional histories affect the brain circuitry. John was bitten by a dog when he was a boy. The bite hurt, and John was frightened. The event became stored in his emotional memory even though, on a conscious level, John had forgotten all about it. Today, when John sees a dog—even a cute puppy—his brain compares the image of the animal with his stored memories. There it finds a match with the memory of "dog" and "getting bitten," which then triggers a feeling of fear. This feeling then affects the cognitive centers in his brain and influences the way John thinks about dogs. Without a doubt, how he reacts to the puppy is a "head" feeling: a judgment that dogs in general are dangerous. John is being controlled by his emotional history—by insecure feelings generated by the head, not the heart.

Of course, these memories do not happen only with dogs and puppies; they happen with all strong emotional imprints. If you've been a victim of violence or abuse, your amygdala can trigger a fearful feeling, then angry thoughts, if someone just gives you a funny look. Your current experiences of people, places, and situations prompt the amygdala to find a match between the past and present. This is not bad. It's a built-in protective survival mechanism. But unless you learn to use your heart to intervene in the process, you will sometimes respond with anger, fear, or anxiety triggered by your emotional histories. The opportunity you have as a human being is that you can develop your heart to change those imprints.

Changing the Old Information

The imprint of Don's rejection, John's dog bite, your parents' emotional traits, or of violence and abuse can be changed—and here is where heart coherence comes in. Coherent heart rhythms transform how your brain functions. Research by Frysinger and Harper in 1990 established that *the cells of the amygdala are synchronized to the heart.* Incoherent heart rhythms tend to activate insecure feelings, while coherent heart rhythms help activate feelings of security which help override negative imprints.

The mechanism of transformation is love. Positive feelings like appreciation, care, and compassion are aspects of love, and they generate coherent heart rhythms. Coherent heart rhythms trigger a transformational process by changing the signals transmitted from your heart to your amygdala, your thalamus (the control center that synchronizes brain activity), and then your frontal lobes.

Heart coherence activates intelligence. Synchronizing your head and your heart facilitates thinking from your higher brain. You perceive more options. Getting your head in sync with your heart allows you to see solutions that you otherwise would not have been able to see and select actions that are best for you and others.

With practice, you can use the coherent power of your heart to imprint a new pattern of security in your amygdala. Each of us has the power to clear patterns that no longer serve us. You can erase an old pattern, just like you can erase an old tape recording. It takes heart intent and practice to rewire your brain, but you will see the mechanism of transformation at work as you use the heart tools.

Choosing Heart Intelligence

It is important to recognize how emotional histories are affecting you and, in many cases, controlling you. Once you realize this, you can choose to become more aware of your mechanical responses and use heart tools to reduce fear, anxiety, frustration, and anger. The heart tools will help you respond more from your heart intelligence as you free yourself from the pull of emotional memories that aren't useful or helpful to you anymore.

What your heart tells you at any time matches your readiness to hear it. Your heart intuition unfolds as you grow in emotional maturity. As you increase your ratio of being "in the heart" versus being "in the head," you'll find new insights for dealing with triggers and releasing emotional histories. You will get to the point where you recognize when you are reacting from your old "head" self, then choose to go to your heart to find your real self.

The Heart Lock-In technique is designed to help you generate and sustain coherence and distinguish between your head voice and your heart voice. To sustain emotional coherence, you focus your attention in the area of your heart and learn to send positive feelings out to others or to yourself. If emotional histories and reactions come up while you do this, you send them love. When thoughts pull you into the head, you bring your focus back to the heart. You keep pulling your energy from the head back down to the heart and build power to stay in your heart.

It is nature's design that you get your head in sync with your deeper heart intent. You can find a new type of fun in listening to your heart as your command center. The fun is in gaining back your power not to go the mechanical way—the old way of the head. When you do fall back, you replace feeling bad about it with feeling compassion for yourself. Compassion will quickly shift you back into emotional coherence. You stop wasting your energy judging yourself or others. You stop those painful feelings churning inside. You release your own energy and power to do the things that matter most to you. You preserve your health and promote happiness in your relationships. While you can't always avoid painful experiences of unkindness or unfairness, you can choose how you handle your emotions. Your choices make all the difference.

✐ *Heart Lock-In Technique*

1. *Gently shift your attention to the area around your heart.*

2. *Shift your breathing so that you are breathing in through the heart and out through the solar plexus.*

3. *Activate a genuine feeling of appreciation or care for someone or something in your life.*

4. *Make a sincere effort to sustain feelings of appreciation or care while directing these feelings toward yourself and others.*

5. *When you catch your mind wandering, gently focus your breathing back through your heart and solar plexus and reconnect with feelings of care or appreciation.*

After you're finished, sincerely sustain your feelings of care and appreciation as long as you can. This will act as a cushion against recurring stress or anxiety.

You will be able to memorize the five steps of the Heart Lock-In technique after a few practices. Then you can just use the Quick Heart Lock-In steps to guide you through the whole technique.

Quick Heart Lock-In Steps

- Focus

- Appreciate

- Sustain

Practice the Heart Lock-In with the aim of going deep inside your heart and staying there for five minutes or longer. It's fine to visualize a person or situation, like a child you love or a place in nature you appreciated, in order to find a sincere feeling or attitude of appreciation, care, or love. But it's important to then let the visualization go and focus on radiating the feeling or attitude through your body or directing the feeling toward others.

Try to keep your focus between your heart and solar plexus to anchor your attention. Observe your tendency to get pulled back to your head. Observe the dynamics inside yourself, then bring your energy back to the heart to lock it in.

After you practice a while, you will open to a greater flow of creative ideas. Write down ideas you'd like to remember and put into action. Then go back to your heart focus. Strengthen the "muscle" that allows you to return to your heart for longer time periods during Heart Lock-Ins. You will build a new foundation for responding differently to anger triggers. The more you practice, the more you increase your power to achieve coherence and transformation.

chapter 6

Building New Reference Points

The tools and techniques you have learned so far for transforming anger—Attitude Breathing, Go to Neutral, and Heart Lock-In—help to refocus your emotions in a positive direction. As you practice these techniques, you build new reference points of inner security to draw on when stress or anger start to take over. You become able to shift quickly out of disordered emotional states—the states that make your heart rhythms incoherent—into more coherent emotional and mental states. You gain access to the power of your deeper intuitive intelligence. But to enjoy the full benefit of these tools and techniques, you need to practice them regularly. You will progress in stages as you build new, positive reference points. When you fall back, don't get mad at yourself or discouraged. Just use the tools to pick yourself back up. You build self-security incrementally, sometimes three steps forward then one step back. As long as you keep using the tools, you will progress and develop inner confidence.

A fourth technique, called Freeze-Frame, is designed to help you take a time-out and get an intuitive perspective at the very moment you're feeling stressed. In basketball, when one team feels the game is getting out of hand, they call a time-out. Why? So they can step back, gain a wider perspective on what's happening, and make adjustments in their strategy to win the game. A time-out also helps the team collect and renew its energies. This is what Freeze-Frame does for you. You use Freeze-Frame to stop incoherence in the moment, assess situations objectively, and find intuitive solutions.

It's called Freeze-Frame because it gives you power to freeze the frame of the movie of your life at that moment. Just like pressing the pause button on your VCR or DVD, you can stop the movie, call time-out, and get a clearer perspective. Then you can edit the "frame," resume the "movie," and create a different outcome.

The first two steps of Freeze-Frame are similar to the first two steps of Go to Neutral, which you learned in chapter 3. The third step of Freeze-Frame helps you increase your coherence and get your heart and brain more in sync. Steps 4 and 5 then train you to ask yourself questions in this synchronized state and sense intuitive responses.

✐ *Freeze-Frame Technique*

1. Take a time-out so that you can temporarily disengage from your thoughts and feelings, especially stressful ones.

2. Shift your focus to the area around your heart. Now feel your breath coming in through your heart and going out through your solar plexus. *Practice breathing this way a few times to ease into the technique.*

3. Make a sincere effort to activate a positive feeling. Allow yourself to feel genuine appreciation or care for some person, some place, or something in your life.

4. Ask yourself what would be an efficient, effective attitude or action that would balance and destress your system. *Your ability to think more clearly and objectively is enhanced based on the increased coherence you've created with steps 2 and 3. The issue can now be viewed from a broader, more balanced perspective. Ask yourself what you can do to help minimize future stress.*

5. Quietly sense any change in perception or feeling, and sustain it as long as you can. *Heart perceptions are often subtle. They gently suggest effective solutions that would be best for you and all concerned.*

After you become practiced in using the Freeze-Frame technique, you will be able to just use the three Quick Freeze-Frame Steps as you move through your day.

Quick Freeze-Frame Steps

- Shift
- Activate
- Sense

Each time you stop going down the stressful track you were on and shift onto a more intuitive track, you'll save loads of energy and time. The conflicts in life won't all stop, but Freeze-Frame will help you respond to those situations more appropriately, improving your chances for a better outcome.

After you practice Freeze-Frame, *ask your heart to give you quicker access to the memory of what your heart intuition has told you,* especially when you need it most. If you sincerely commit to what your heart says, you will often get intuitive reminders or alarm signals just when you need them to help you follow through.

Laura shares her story of how this has worked for her:

*I had been practicing the Freeze-Frame technique to
deal with my anger for a few months, when one
evening I went to my mother's house to visit. When I
got there I could feel a strong tension in the
household. My mother looked like she had been crying.
I asked her what had happened, and she told me she'd
had an argument with my stepfather. She was
standing at the top of the stairs while they were
yelling at each other, and he pushed at her chest while
making a point. Well, it was enough of a push to
send her tumbling down the stairs.*

*My blood instantly started to boil. How dare he
lay a finger on her! I didn't need to hear any more.
All I knew was I needed to straighten him out. I'm a
small person, but I feel ten feet tall and capable of
taking on the Hulk when I'm angry.*

*My stepfather was packing his car to leave, and
just then he walked in the front door. I charged, like
an angry bull, toward him. But as I got right up next
to him, I just passed him by, went out the front door,
and stood on the porch and instinctively did the
Freeze-Frame technique.*

*In that suspended moment of time, I remembered
to go to my heart and not act from anger but to
assess the situation from a more intelligent place. I
clearly saw that adding my anger to the situation
would not help my mother feel comforted, it would not
help my stepfather, and it would not help me deal
with the situation in a mature and reasonable way.
After I used the Freeze-Frame technique, I went back
inside, much more in control. I heard my stepfather's
side of the story. I strongly and calmly told him to
finish packing and to leave. The rest of the evening I*

*was able to spend with my mother, helping her gather
her own clarity about the situation.*

*For me this was a life-changing experience.
Anger was always a problem for me before I learned
how to use the Freeze-Frame technique. If not for this
technique, no doubt I would have verbally and, likely,
physically attacked my stepfather without thinking.
Now, several years later, I continue to use the
Freeze-Frame technique, and my reactive anger is
very much in control. In fact, I can't recall the last
time I had a fit of anger. That makes me feel great
about who I've become.*

Using Freeze-Frame on small issues first will help build
the foundation you'll need to tackle bigger issues when they
arise. Practice is the key. Create a Freeze-Frame worksheet to
get yourself started. A Freeze-Frame worksheet works like
training wheels on a bike, guiding you in the shift from head
reaction to intuitive perspective, until you can use the technique without a worksheet. By writing down your perceptions, you clarify the difference between your head reaction
and your heart perspective. When you write down your
heart's response and review it a number of times, you are
more likely to follow through with what your intuitive heart
tells you.

✎ *Freeze-Frame Worksheet*

1. *Pick a current stressful situation that gets you angry. Don't
pick your biggest trigger. You're just getting started, so you
want to begin with something small and build your
confidence. Write "Stressful Situation" on a piece of paper or
in your notebook, and jot down a few words describing it.*

2. *Now write "Head Reaction," and spend a few moments
considering your thoughts and feelings about the situation.*

How do you typically react? Maybe you've been feeling frustrated, burned out, or hopeless. Maybe you think the other person gets in your way and is to blame. Be honest. This is a private exercise. Write down your responses.

3. *Now go through the steps of the Freeze-Frame technique. Don't expect a dramatic insight the first time. You might sense a subtle shift in perspective or a confirmation of what your heart already knows about the situation.*

4. *On your worksheet, write "Intuitive Perspective." Jot down any insights or changes in perception or feeling you received in steps 4 and 5 of the Freeze-Frame technique. Don't edit the insights, just write them down and look at them. Heart-intelligent perspectives are often accompanied by a feeling of ease or peace and are often very simple. At times, they can even seem too simple.*

5. *Read your head reaction again, then read your intuitive perspective again. See if you notice any difference in the quality, tone, and feeling of the responses. Write down one word to describe the head reaction and one word to describe the intuitive response.*

6. *Take a step back, and ask yourself which seems more logical, the head reaction or the heart response. Most people are surprised to see that the head can be more emotional and illogical than the heart.*

7. *Now ask yourself if you noticed a change in your stress level. Even if you didn't get a solution, your stress level might have decreased, and that's worth a lot. You are balancing your emotions and nervous system just by practicing.*

8. *Write "Positive Reference Points" on your piece of paper. If you noticed a positive shift toward a new neutral, or a shift in perspective or in attitude, write it down. Write down the attitude, image, or memory you focused on in step 3 to activate a positive feeling. This can become a new reference point or*

reference state to go back to as you practice Go to Neutral, Attitude Breathing, Heart Lock-In, and Freeze-Frame. As you accumulate positive reference points to refer back to (and eventually default to instead of defaulting to your same old negative references), you build a platform of sustainable coherence in your system. Honor and value your new reference points to anchor them in your system.

9. *Make a list of other things in your life — people, pets, places, events, insights — that bring you a genuine feeling of appreciation or care. You can use any positive experience as a reference point to boost coherence.*

How People Are Using Freeze-Frame

Many psychologists, clinicians, and coaches are teaching Freeze-Frame to their clients to help them transform anger and make better decisions. One of the most common questions psychologists ask us is how long it will take to see shifts in their clients who use Freeze-Frame to transform anger. Psychologists find that angry people can often be self-righteous and unsympathetic about the effect of their anger on other people. As Dr. Norman Rosenthal states in *The Emotional Revolution* (2002), "they think it's everyone else's problem—obnoxious boss, difficult wife, incompetent employees." So often clients reluctantly go to therapists because they have been told to by a supervisor, a doctor, their spouse, or a judge. Having clients use the Freeze-Frame technique and worksheet often helps them see for themselves the truth of what others are saying. Dr. Jim Kowal, a counselor at a traumatic stress center, had several men referred to him (by their wives) for road rage. The men had gotten very upset while driving, and their wives were concerned that something terrible would happen. Dr. Kowal taught the men the

Freeze-Frame technique, and each man got over his road rage quite quickly and now can drive normally.

One of the chief attributes of the HeartMath interventions is the speed with which they work. Jasmina J. Agrillo, a licensed HeartMath provider, explains:

> *Whenever a HeartMath tool is sincerely applied, there is an immediate shift. I will coach the client around recognizing the shift. Sometimes his or her mind comes in later, doubting the shift. Because the tools are so simple and easy to practice, self-doubt can easily happen, as the mind likes complexity and having to figure things out. It's fun to coach a client on recognizing his or her own "shifts" and building new reference points with them. Once they start identifying their heart shifts, they feel more confidence, and that inspires them to create more shifts. Then it starts to become a habit to go to the heart to return to a state of balance. A daily practice seems to support the long-term shift needed to retrain neural circuitry around anger responses. I see a shift happen more rapidly and in a bigger way once my client sees it too, without me having to coach him or her on it.*

Jasmina gives an example of how her clients learn to use the heart tools to respond constructively from a place of compassion rather than becoming trapped in the usual anger response and its consequences. She describes her client Tim, who used Freeze-Frame successfully before Jasmina had even finished teaching him the technique. "At that time I hadn't officially instructed him on the entire Freeze-Frame technique. I wasn't planning to do that until our third session in order to allow him to get used to the steps gradually. He related the following story to me on our second session together."

Tim's Story

Tim has been his younger brother's legal guardian for twelve years. His brother suffered permanent brain damage as a result of complications from anesthesia while undergoing a surgical procedure. One of the effects of the brain damage is that his brother is often unable to control his impulses. He says and does things that anger Tim greatly.

In this recent incident, Tim's brother asked Tim, in a verbally insulting way, to get out of his house because he was expecting a guest. Tim's typical reaction to this would have been to verbally insult his brother back, storm out of his brother's house, and not communicate for a time after that. This time he remembered "to not let the mind go on the familiar route, knowing where that would lead me." He focused his awareness and breath in the area of his heart and then was able to respond in a clear, constructive way. He remained very conscious of the shift to the heart while communicating with his brother. During his communication, he felt a compassionate understanding for both their predicaments. "I stopped the train wreck!" he told Jasmina. "For the first time in over twelve years, I was able to positively control the situation, feel at peace, not waste my energy, and not have to go through all the apologies later."

In hindsight, after learning all the steps of the Freeze-Frame technique, Tim realized that he achieved the positive benefits of shifting into a place of neutrality in that situation. The first two steps of Freeze-Frame, which Jasmina had taught him, showed him how to Go to Neutral. Tim continues to experience a growing sense of peace, calmness, and clarity in his life. As he likes to describe it, "The cobwebs are being cleared from my brain."

Simeon Nartoomid, a minister and licensed HeartMath provider, also uses Freeze-Frame to help people identify what's behind their anger. "When we are filled with anger, it helps immensely to recognize we often have an underlying fear that drives the anger," says Simeon. "I find there are two basic responses to fear: (1) immobilization, being 'frozen with fear,' and (2) aggression, which often uses justified anger as its motivator." Simeon has found that the Freeze-Frame technique helps people intuitively uncover the fear if it is not readily apparent, and then get to the source of the anger. Using Freeze-Frame in combination with Heart Lock-In, they can effectively dissipate the stored anger. Simeon recommends the following practice:

1. *Do the first three steps of Freeze-Frame to either discover the fear or help it abate. If you are using the technique to discover the fear, then use it a second time to help the fear abate. If discovery reveals nothing, then just move forward on the premise that fear exists. You'll be taking an indirect approach to the anger, like walking a spiral labyrinth toward its center.*

2. *In step 3 of Freeze-Frame, shift into appreciation of the fear as a protective mechanism that actually seeks to help you.*

3. *From the state of appreciation you reached in step 3 of Freeze-Frame, shift to step 3 of the Heart Lock-In. Focus on creating a genuine feeling of appreciation and care for someone or something positive in your life. Try to really feel the emotions of appreciation and care, and send that appreciation out to the fear and also to the person or situation that has angered you.*

You can try these approaches for yourself. We suggest using a Freeze-Frame worksheet as your coach. Reading what you wrote can provide you with more objectivity. You can also use a Freeze-Frame worksheet for any type of creative problem solving or decision making. If you have a tough choice to make and you're not sure which way to go, use the worksheet to gain intuitive perspectives. If you're still uncertain, rest your head a while and use Go to Neutral, then Attitude Breathing or Heart Lock-In to give your heart a chance to work. Increased clarity often comes within a short period of time if you stay in the heart. Some issues take time, but your Freeze-Frame worksheet can show you a next step or attitude to hold until you have clarity.

Using Freeze-Frame in Action

After a little practice, you will find that Freeze-Frame can be a one-minute-or-less power tool for transforming anger and other stressful emotions into efficient and effective action. Eventually, you will be able to use just the Quick Freeze-Frame Steps: Shift (to the heart), Activate (a positive emotion or reference), and Sense (intuitively what to do). You can Freeze-Frame anytime or anywhere—in the middle of an argument or a staff meeting or a traffic jam—and tap into your innate intelligence. Some people use the Freeze-Frame technique a dozen or more times a day to step back from a problem, get in sync, and allow their perspective to widen. Jim, an executive at a Fortune 100 company, says, "I probably use Freeze-Frame a hundred times on some days to keep me sane. I don't know where I'd be without it."

Even children find it easy to use the Freeze-Frame technique to transform anger in action. Here's how some of the children we've worked with describe their experiences.

> *The reason for doing the Freeze-Frame is to shift from a negative emotion to a positive emotion and see how your heart reads the situation. The first time I used Freeze-Frame was in my ice hockey game while I was arguing with a referee. I stopped and I asked myself if this was worth getting a penalty over. The benefits of using Freeze-Frame for me are it helps me control my anger and I can take a break from all the stress I have had that day.*
>
> — A., tenth grade

This has worked to get me to control my anger. I have already gotten angry at my friends and the Freeze-Frame has kept me from blowing up in their faces. Thank you so much.

—R., seventh grade

HeartMath has really helped me a lot. I was in a fight with one of my friends but then I Freeze-Framed. I found out what the problem was and then my friend and I both attacked the problem instead of each other and now we're best friends. Thank you!

—A., seventh grade

When you take a minute and Freeze-Frame, all the stress and anger just seem to go away. Instead of listening to your head, which will tell you to fight back probably, you listen to your heart and give a simple "I'm sorry!"

—G., seventh grade

Slowing the Galloping Mind

When time pressures abound, the mind's tendency is to either procrastinate to avoid the pressures or race faster to stay ahead of them. A racing mind can be hard to slow down, but the Freeze-Frame technique can help. Amanda's story is typical. She says,

I'm up in the morning, and it's off to the racetrack. My mind goes and goes, then when I want to have a peaceful meal or conversation or get a good night's sleep, it's hard to slow it down. This can interfere with my ability to focus the next day and can make me feel like I have an attention-deficit disorder. It also makes me irritable and quick tempered.

Underneath the galloping mind are feelings that fuel the runaway momentum. Remember that feelings are quicker than thoughts and take control without you knowing it. Your mind has to slow down in order for you to intuitively sense what your emotions are doing. This is especially true if you are prone to anger. As Ron Potter-Efron says in *Angry All the Time,* "Anger is a hard habit to break. The most important thing you'll need to do is to slow down the whole process" (1994).

"Soon after I started using the Freeze-Frame technique," explains Amanda,

> *I was able to slow my mind long enough to let my heart show me what was underneath me living in overdrive. I saw how my fear of not being liked if I didn't get everything done was keeping me running and trigger-quick to anger. I get irritated with anyone who tries to slow me down because it gets in my way. Once I saw how this fear of not being liked was actually pushing people away and making people not like me, I decided to keep using Freeze-Frame to slow my mind down and connect with people more. Irritation and anger subsided, and life is much more enjoyable. I also get done more of what's important and I let the busywork go.*

You can "slow-frame" situations or issues with Freeze-Frame while you're on the move. "Slow-frame" means slowing down your mind and emotions and drawing them into your heart so you can bring them into coherence. Slow-frame slows the galloping mind as you draw your mental energies down into your heart and shift to a heart reference. It allows the head to get in sync with the heart before you react to incoming data or perceptions. You are always emotionally evaluating information. If you're out of sync with your heart, your brain can interpret the information as stressful and react with frustration or disappointment before you have a chance to consider the situation intelligently. When you slow-frame to a heart reference, you can find a more coherent response. Slow-frame in the heart shows you more options. It creates the opportunity for your heart intelligence to come in and remind you of what you may have realized before and already committed to do.

You can regulate your runaway mind at any time by pulling your mental and emotional energies into your heart with the intention of slowing down your response, just as you would slow the speed of a video to see it frame by frame. Practice Freeze-Frame, then slowly draw your energies into your heart. Breathe in through the heart and out through the solar plexus to ground your energy. Keep slowing your energies and pulling them into your heart as you move through your day. This will build your power. You can also add Attitude Breathing and breathe an attitude of care into your mind, emotions, and body as you regroup. You will transform incoherent emotional energy and instate a new habit of moving through your day with more emotional coherence and harmony. Guaranteed—you'll feel better and be more effective.

Go through the steps of the Freeze-Frame technique a few times a day, even if you aren't feeling stress, just to develop your power to get in the heart and shift to intuition. Practice sending out appreciation and care a few times each day, whether or not you feel angry. As you practice the different heart tools and build new reference points, you will learn when to use which one and how to combine them creatively for the best results. You will be able to maintain a new centeredness and poise so you can navigate through life more smoothly and effectively.

chapter 7

Sustaining the Shift: Conserving Your Emotional Energy

Now that you've learned how to recognize your anger triggers and transform your reactions, you will want to sustain and build on the shifts you've made. A practice program is the key. Practice Go to Neutral, Attitude Breathing, and Freeze-Frame several times as you go about your day, *whether or not anything triggers your anger*. Practice them to program them into your memory and your neural circuitry. Practice them as preventive maintenance, to conserve and increase your emotional energy. You will start to experience significant improvements in your energy levels and attitude. Practice the Heart Lock-In technique several times a week to learn to go deeper in your heart and sustain your ability to respond from the heart.

Two additional skills will help you fine-tune your use of the tools and achieve a more coherent way of living. First, become more conscious of how you spend your emotional energy throughout a day to prevent emotional drains from happening. Second, become aware of when you *overpersonalize* a situation, judging yourself to be good or bad. Let's take them one at a time.

How Do You Spend Your Emotional Energy?

Becoming aware of how you spend your emotional energy every day can help you identify when your emotional energy is being drained. An emotional drain occurs whenever you experience a negative emotion like irritation or frustration. An emotional drain occurs whenever you react to something as a "take-away"—a disappointment, a feeling that something is unfair, a judgment against yourself, a fear of loss, or worry. An emotional drain also occurs whenever you get too far out of balance from positive emotions—overexcitement, overstimulation, overworking your mind, and so forth. All of these can lead to incoherence. The goal is to experience all of your feelings, but shift back to balance before they become drains and deficits. This will increase your emotional enjoyment and bring you more intuitive insights. If you're draining away emotional energy, you can lose new insights you've gained. They're gone—poof!—and you may forget you ever had them. Insights and positive emotional experiences are your emotional assets. They need coherence to be sustained.

It is possible to get an objective look at your emotional assets and deficits over a day or a week. Just as you would keep a balance sheet of assets and deficits if you were running a business, you can keep a balance sheet of your emotional income and expenses. *Use the balance sheet exercise to gain insight about at how you're running your internal business—the business of your emotions, mind, and heart. Once you get a clearer look at your emotional assets and deficits, you can apply the heart tools and techniques to prevent deficits from recurring and transform them more quickly when they do. You can also use the tools to appreciate your assets, both in the sense of feeling grateful for them and in the sense of increasing them.*

🖉 Asset/Deficit Balance Sheet

1. Take a sheet of paper or a page in your journal, and divide it in half, top and bottom. In the top half, write "Assets." In the bottom half, write "Deficits."

2. Under *Assets,* list the positive events, conversations, and interactions of the past few days — things that made you happy and gave you energy. List as many assets as you can think of, feeling appreciation for each asset as you go. Notice how conscious you were of each asset when it occurred and write down how it made you feel. Also list any *ongoing* assets in your life — the overall quality of your friends, family, living and working environments, and so forth.

3. Under *Deficits,* list issues, conflicts, and events during that same period that were negative or draining. Write down how they made you feel. Also list events that started out as assets but turned into energy drains, like a conversation with your daughter that was enjoyable at first but turned into a full-blown argument, or a party that was enjoyable until you let yourself get overstimulated and felt cranky and exhausted.

4. As you make your lists, consider the effects on family, work, and personal balance, and the downstream consequences of each event. After listing assets and deficits, step back and — from the heart — compare your lists. Notice which deficits could have been neutralized or turned into assets *at the time,* had you stopped long enough to gain a wider perspective. Evaluate which deficits could still be transformed into assets. Study the

ratio of assets to deficits, and look for repeating patterns. Write down your insights or conclusions.

Improving Your Bottom Line

Appreciate your assets. You may be taking them for granted. You increase the value of your assets by being more conscious of them. You can use Attitude Breathing and Heart Lock-In to add appreciation to your assets. Consider what actions you can take to feel and express more appreciation.

Start using the heart tools on your deficits and notice what happens. Decide which tool you think might be most appropriate for each situation — Go to Neutral, Attitude Breathing, Freeze-Frame, or Heart Lock-In — and write that tool next to the deficit. Try the tools, and see if you don't gain valuable new insights. If similar deficits repeat on your balance sheet and you're not sure which tool to use, do a Freeze-Frame worksheet to gain an intuitive perspective on how to stop the drain. Often an intuitive answer for one situation is also the answer to other similar situations.

As an example, here is Melissa's balance sheet:

Assets:

- Daughter gave me a surprise compliment — felt great

- Mother-in-law transferred to better nursing home — big relief

- Got angry at husband for being late again — used Go to Neutral and Attitude Breathing — helped a lot — prevented argument

Deficits:

- Got angry at my boss — fumed for hours and wasn't productive

- Got irritated and snapped at daughter — she left and stayed out past curfew — felt horrible

- Trapped in traffic—went into rage—rear-ended a BMW—will cost me—worried about that for hours

- Drank too much—felt awful—got headache

Note that under Assets, Melissa listed getting angry at her husband and using two heart tools to prevent an argument. A situation that could have resulted in a big deficit was turned into an asset *because she transformed her anger and saved so much energy.*

Doing an Asset-Deficit Balance Sheet a couple of times a week can give you a lot of clarity about situations in which you could benefit from using the heart tools. It will also help you develop a healthy objectivity about your anger. As you keep a balance sheet and use the heart tools to grow assets and transform deficits, you will no longer view emotional reactions as good or bad. Instead, you will begin to see them more objectively as effective or ineffective. You will see more clearly how energy drains from ineffective reactions have downstream consequences. They wreak havoc on your emotional, mental, and physical health and on your relationships and work productivity. You will also see how using the heart tools can quickly build back your emotional energy and restore your energy reserves.

Overpersonalization

A second key skill for sustaining your emotional coherence is learning not to overpersonalize your deficits, since this just makes the energy drain worse.

Overpersonalizing is judging yourself as good or bad depending on how you reacted to a situation or how someone reacted to you. It's human to overpersonalize, but it's one of the biggest energy drains of all. Overpersonalization can keep you stuck in head reactions and runaway emotions for hours or days. An undercurrent of roiling thoughts and emotions about "how it went" or "what you should have said" can go on while you work, play with your children, or try to conduct your normal activities.

Overpersonalizing can hurt the heart. Many people feel physical pain in the area of the heart from repressed hurts, fears, or anger due to overpersonalization. When you exaggerate your personal role in—or responsibility for—a situation, you block the bigger picture and you can't feel any hope. Life seems unfair, so you become a victim, and that can lead to depression.

It is easy to overpersonalize, because it's human nature. Almost everybody does it. It's so common that it causes an emotional telepathy of overpersonalization. You can feel the heavy energy in the air. While you're overpersonalizing a situation that didn't go well, the other parties involved are probably doing the same, draining untold amounts of energy without resolution. Overpersonalizing keeps people self-centered and focused on getting the best outcome for themselves, often at the expense of others.

A key aspect of heart intelligence is that it helps you to depersonalize issues so that you can let go of them and move on. This frees up energy to see a more intelligent response or to do better next time. Dr. Joseph McCaffrey, a surgeon, told us how he used Freeze-Frame to deal with a situation that not only could have reflected badly on him but also could have meant life or death to a patient.

> *When an anesthesiologist told me that he wouldn't give his high-risk patient anesthesia because the patient hadn't been evaluated properly, I almost lost it! This was the second such incident with him in less than a week. I was ready to blow up. I just about had my finger on the anesthesiologist's chest when I decided to use the Freeze-Frame technique. I froze my anger, started breathing through the area of my heart, and reflected on a good memory that was strong*

enough to evoke feelings of appreciation. As my agitation cleared, I realized that the anesthesiologist was as interested in taking good care of the patient as I was. Keeping that common ground in mind, I was able to bring the anesthesiologist around to my point of view — without exploding. I could have been the typical obnoxious surgeon, but that wouldn't have made for a very collegial relationship.

Joe told us that if he had blown up, he would have felt terrible later and blamed himself. Can you remember a time when you got angry, blamed yourself, and then told the person "I'm sorry" over and over? After all, it was your fault. When you overpersonalize, you keep feeling bad and believe that if you blame and shame yourself, maybe others will still approve of you. Blame and shame are the end result of overpersonalization. You keep yourself victimized. That doesn't feel good, so after a while you look for something or someone else to blame. Maybe you blame your parents for how they treated you when you were five years old, but that doesn't help either.

Instead of victimizing yourself, use one of the techniques you've learned. When you tune in to the intelligence of your heart, it will tell you, "What's done is done. Forgive and let go of it. You, your parents, and other people all did the best they knew how, given their own emotional natures and histories." The heart tools give you the power to forgive. You can do now what you couldn't do before.

As you use the heart tools to depersonalize situations, your heart intelligence will give you a whole new package of insights for dealing with blame and shame. You'll also find a new type of enjoyment in listening to your heart as your command and control center. The fun is in seeing your power not to cave in to the tendency to overpersonalize.

Connie tells how she used Attitude Breathing in a moment of overpersonalizing. One day she was watching

Oprah with some friends and saw a woman who seemed like a control freak. Connie found herself identifying with the woman, since she knew she herself had a strong tendency to want to be in control of things and to feel that if she's not in control, something bad might happen. "I found myself wanting to defend the woman while everyone else watching the show was criticizing her," says Connie. "I started to overpersonalize the situation, seeing myself in the woman and feeling bad about myself." Connie began to feel that everyone in the room was thinking of her when they saw the control freak, and she wanted to shrink away. She kept thinking, "I'm just like her, always wanting to tell others what to do to make sure it's done right. Or when something goes wrong, I want to run right out and fix it. I get uptight and short-tempered until I can fix what went wrong."

But then Connie noticed that she was shaming herself internally. She had learned Attitude Breathing and decided to use it while watching the rest of the show. She practiced breathing love and compassion through her heart, for the woman on the show and for herself. "I was amazed at how my 'feeling bad' lifted and I was able to see that I was overpersonalizing. No one was looking at me. I felt free." If Connie hadn't used Attitude Breathing, her overpersonalizing might have ruined her whole afternoon.

Check the deficits you listed on your balance sheet. How long did they go on? See if some of them weren't due to overpersonalizing and making an already stressful situation worse. Overpersonalizing can lead to distorted and exaggerated perceptions like the following:

Catastrophizing. Exaggerating the harmful effect of something that happens to you. For example, your husband offers you mild criticism, and you're sure he's seeing someone else.

Absolutism. All-or-nothing thinking. For example, if you're not a *perfect* parent—if you make what you think is a mistake — then you think you're a *terrible* parent and you mentally beat yourself up for hours.

Mental filtering. Focusing on the bad while screening out the positive. For example, your boss praises a report you wrote but criticizes how you formatted it. All you remember is the criticism, and you stay angry for hours. That anger energy accumulates in your system and makes you skew future situations with similar mental filtering.

Look at your deficits, and see if any of them bring up issues of what's fair or unfair. Can you sense a feeling of pain or hurt in your heart as you look at these situations? If so, go to your heart and breathe love and compassion to yourself or others. Use the heart tools to find your deeper intelligence and common sense. When you overpersonalize, don't make a big deal out of it. Use Go to Neutral to stop the drain, then Attitude Breathing or Heart Lock-In to stabilize the new attitude, and Freeze-Frame to intuitively sense what to do next.

To transform the pain, hurt, shame, or fear in your heart, you need to add the power of compassion. Through your heart, you can bring your emotional nature into balance and find new hope.

chapter 8

The Power of Compassion

Compassion has been referred to throughout this book as a tool that can shift your emotions and your heart rhythms into more coherence. Compassion is a core value of the heart or an aspect of love, as are appreciation and care. The heart's core values are qualities and feelings that bring more optimal functioning to human physiology and facilitate greater harmony and well-being. Having compassion for yourself and others is essential to transforming anger.

Compassion gives you the power to care about yourself and others without getting stressed out. When your care for people, work, issues, and things in your life causes you stress, it becomes *overcare*. Overcare creates incoherence in your heart rhythms. Overcare is deceptive because you really do care—about a project you're working on, your son's grades, having enough money to pay the bills—yet your head has turned your care into frustration, worry, or anger. Overcare happens when you overpersonalize situations, becoming stressed about how someone will react to you or what someone said to you, or becoming too attached to how something will turn out. Overcare starts with real care, but turns into emotional incoherence and stress. It blocks you from seeing solutions and keeps you feeling frustrated and angry, or leads you into depression.

Compassion is the antidote for overcare. It helps you see appropriate next steps. *If you find yourself getting worried, frustrated, or angry from overcare, use Attitude Breathing and breathe an attitude of compassion in through your heart and out through your solar plexus. A compassionate attitude can be directed toward yourself, other people, even world events.* Activating the power of compassion will help stabilize your care. Compassion acts like a soothing balm to your nervous system. Sending out compassion and balanced care is one of the fastest ways to depersonalize situations and gain more clarity.

Compassion builds your sense of security. Compassion helps you move through life with a new feeling of ease, and decreases the strength and frequency of your emotional triggers. When you judge or blame yourself or others, you only stoke frustration and anger. That's because judgment and blame typically cover up an underlying lack of security.

Your immune system and health are also empowered as you practice adding more compassion and care. Compassion boosts the immune system, while anger suppresses the immune response for up to six hours following an episode of anger (Rein, Atkinson, and McCraty 1995).

Anger as a Cover-Up

Compassion helps you see that frustration, anger, and rage are often a cover-up for other unresolved feelings of hurt, betrayal, guilt, and blame. To uncover and then transform what anger is covering up, you need the power of compassion. *The "Looking Beneath Anger" exercise will help you identify what may be underlying your anger triggers. Practice the power of compassion as you do this exercise. Use Go to Neutral and Attitude Breathing of compassion as you answer the questions. It will help you feel safe as unresolved issues stored in your neural circuitry resurface. Breathe compassion in through the heart and out through the solar plexus to release stored emotional energy and depersonalize the issues. No one wants to relive the pain of the past. With the power of compassion, you can release those stored feelings and gain a more neutral understanding.*

✎ Looking Beneath Anger

1. *On a piece of paper or in your journal, write down the ways you react when you are angry. Do you do any of the following?*

   - don't admit that you're angry
   - sulk or pout
   - avoid people
   - snap at people
   - act mean to others
   - intimidate or bully others to get your way
   - manipulate others to get your way
   - become sarcastic
   - yell and swear
   - throw things
   - overeat or overdrink
   - find fault with everything
   - think about ways to get even
   - explode
   - become violent
   - add fuel to your anger with more negative thoughts
   - hold in your anger until something makes you "lose it"

2. *Consider what's underneath. Sincerely ask your heart which of the following emotions you could be covering up with your anger:*

- worry
- fear
- guilt
- hurt
- disappointment
- embarrassment
- jealousy
- resignation
- hopelessness
- depression

Think of a time when you became angry in order to hide your true feelings, and write about it briefly. Did your anger help or hurt you in the situation? Explain.

When you find yourself becoming angry, Freeze-Frame or slow-frame and ask yourself,

- Am I hurt, jealous, or disappointed? Why?
- What is frustrating me?
- What am I afraid of?
- What do I really want?

3. *Think of an old emotional memory that comes up and still triggers anger, and write it down. What underlying feelings does this situation trigger in you? List the underlying feelings. They could be any of the following, or others not listed here.*

- insecurity
- guilt
- hurt
- disappointment
- embarrassment
- jealousy
- resentment

- unlovable

What images or thoughts generally follow those feelings? Next to the feelings, write down the images or thoughts that follow.

Now, if you look back at the deficits you listed on your Asset/Deficit Balance Sheet in chapter 7, you'll probably find some of your covered-up emotions contributing to your deficits. Continue to use Go to Neutral or Attitude Breathing of compassion to help release them.

Over the next few days, when you find yourself becoming frustrated or angry, use the Freeze-Frame technique and ask yourself what's underneath. In order to *transform* the emotions you uncover, it's important to keep checking in with your feelings during the day. It only takes a second to pause and ask yourself, "What's going on? What am I feeling?" Be honest with yourself about whatever you are feeling. If something is bothering or disturbing you, realize you are draining emotional energy. Getting frustrated will drain more energy, while shoving your feelings back under will keep the energy locked up until the next trigger.

To transform whatever emotion you find underneath, send compassion and care to yourself in order to befriend the feeling. That will help free up the locked energy and bring more coherence. If you push the uncomfortable feeling away, it will remain as an undercurrent. Look fear or discomfort in the face and send care or compassion to the part of yourself that is afraid or uncomfortable. Embrace the discomfort with your heart. Pause to remind yourself again that it's okay. Your feelings are standard human reactions. Have compassion for yourself, then pick yourself up and go back to the heart again without overpersonalizing the feelings. Use Attitude Breathing or Freeze-Frame to transform the energy and get more intuitive clarity. Understand that transformation of unresolved emotions is achieved in stages of release and insight, not all at once. Anchor whatever insights you gain through Attitude Breathing and act on what your heart tells you.

Heart Vulnerability

Often people avoid feelings because they're afraid of becoming vulnerable, getting pulled into an emotional sinkhole they won't easily get out of. There are different types of vulnerability. Vulnerability to your stored-up emotions can take you down the tubes. Vulnerability to other people's emotions can also drain you. A third type of vulnerability, *vulnerability to your heart*, gives you the power to manage the other two.

Being heart vulnerable is not being sentimental or mushy. It's not trying to do good and letting others walk on you or allowing their feelings to pull you down. Being heart vulnerable is staying solidly centered in your heart while you *feel* what's really going on and *listen* to your commonsense heart intelligence.

Feelings have to be addressed, or they'll hold back progress in many areas of your life. Being heart vulnerable allows you to notice your feelings as they move through you, hopefully before they cascade into anger or rage. When you notice and feel what's real, you can add compassion to the feelings. If you overpersonalize what comes up with disappointment, hurt, or guilt, you'll respond from your head, not your heart. It's only human to overpersonalize, but that doesn't bring transformation. You have to stay centered in your heart and use the power of compassion as uncomfortable feelings come up. Then your heart intelligence will help you address them.

The heart gets a bad rap because people associate it with insecurity or heartbreak. But that's not the coherent heart we're talking about. Insecurity is a head feeling that leads to incoherent heart rhythms. When people become emotionally vulnerable out of insecurity, they pout, get demanding, and are likely to feel hurt. That's because their care has strings attached. They want things to turn out a certain way. Then when they don't get what they want, they get angry.

Mush and insecurity are not openheartedness. True openheartedness or heart vulnerability is adding love, compassion, appreciation, or forgiveness—not to get something back, but to stay centered in the heart. Heart vulnerability can transform insecurity into more security, and bring you clearer messages from your intuition.

Your intuition matures as you mature emotionally. *Start by being more heart vulnerable with yourself. Feel what's really going on inside you. This is not a posture you assume; it's simply an agreement to listen more deeply to your own heart. Focus your attention in your heart and ask yourself, "What am I really feeling right now?" Or, "What am I feeling about this meeting that's been dragging on and on? . . . the way my son just spoke to my wife? . . . this upcoming conversation?" If you're not sure what you're feeling, ask yourself more specifically, "Am I feeling fear, hurt, disappointment, or numbness?" Keep your focus of attention in your heart to sense intuitively what's going on.*

Heart vulnerability gives you the key to see what anger might be covering up. You'll become aware of underlying feelings and attitudes that have been shaping your reactions and motivating your decisions without your even knowing it. Then you can use the heart tools you've learned to bring more emotional coherence to those feelings and sense intuitive next steps.

Quite often, people already know what feelings underlie their anger. They know it long before they become heart vulnerable enough to admit it. They may have heard their heart intuition on what to do to help release the underlying feelings. They may even have had strong intentions to do what their heart said, but they couldn't follow through. People revert to the way of the head and to their same old reactions when they are afraid of becoming emotionally vulnerable. They fear what others might think of them or what might happen if they listen to the heart. They're afraid that they'll be criticized or get stepped on. Or afraid they won't get what they want. But these fears are all standard emotional projections and head reactions. Heart vulnerability is listening to what your *heart* wants, without the mind filtering the heart's message to get what the *mind* wants. Responding from the head and not staying open in the heart is one of the biggest causes of emotional pain and regret. You have the power to change that.

Scott and Andy's story shows what happens when you close down your heart. Scott and Andy were friends and business partners. They'd spent many an enjoyable evening relaxing over cocktails, talking about personal and business issues. But then Scott went through a very difficult family time, and Andy told him he couldn't take hearing about it anymore and just wanted a business relationship.

Soon after, their business relationship started to deteriorate. Scott made business decisions that infuriated Andy, while Scott felt Andy was being manipulative and trying to marginalize Scott's role in the company. Things got worse, with each suspecting the other was out to get him, until legal letters were exchanged. Just as the two men were about to enter irreversible legal action, they agreed to talk matters over with an executive coach who was a friend to both. The coach had them use the HeartMath tools to retrace their steps and see what their anger was covering up. Andy became heart vulnerable and admitted that things started to go wrong when he closed off his heart to Scott. Scott was heart vulnerable and was able to tell Andy how his actions had affected him. This was the first authentic communication they'd had in a long time.

It takes a lot of energy to keep emotions covered up and suppress painful feelings churning inside. Things will happen in life that are extremely unfair, unkind, and hurtful.

Through practicing heart vulnerability, you can prevent these experiences from becoming new buried histories or reinforcing old histories. Heart vulnerability is the doorway to intuition and honesty with yourself. With heart vulnerability, intuition has a chance to appear. You have to stay heart vulnerable to anchor yourself in heart intelligence and make better choices in the future.

Finding Your Rhythm through Resistance

You will find it easier to move through obstacles and resistances in life as you practice real heart vulnerability. You'll connect with people on a more authentic level and feel more in sync with yourself. Remember the image in chapter 5 of trying to make your way through a crowded airport? You were running late for your plane but had to move at different speeds depending on the obstacles in your way. You had to slow down when it was crowded, then speed up but not run or you might collide with someone coming the opposite way. When you used a tool to stay centered in your heart, you found a rhythm that allowed you to move and flow around the obstacles.

It's the same in life. It doesn't matter how big you feel your anger problem is or how many obstacles you run into during a day; using the heart, you can move through them in a new way. You'll learn to dance through life instead of feeling like there's no way you'll make it to the gate.

Finding a rhythm through resistances requires listening to your heart as you move through your day. Resistance can come from your own thoughts and emotions, from other people (who may not be doing what you want), or from external obstacles (traffic snarls, computer crashes, bills piling up, and so forth). Sustaining coherence when you meet up with these obstacles takes tuning to the heart for guidance. If your mind is in overdrive or hell-bent on getting its way, the last thing it wants is to slow down and listen to the heart. You have to counter this mind resistance with heart strength. Focus in the heart and breathe through the heart, sending out an attitude of compassion, care, or appreciation. Once you feel more heart coherence or peace, your mind will ease up and resistance will go away.

If you don't have enough coherence in your day-to-day life, you can feel out of rhythm, or out of sync, a lot of the time. Adding the power of compassion with Attitude Breathing will help you regain your rhythm. It takes heart earnest effort to use Attitude Breathing while you are under pressure. At first it can feel like starting up one of those old gas lawn mowers. You have you to pull the cord over and over to get it going, and you have to find a rhythm between cranks. With Attitude Breathing you're trying to reset an old mechanical response. Breathing a new attitude for a while sets a new rhythm in motion. With practice, your new rhythm will become automatic, and you will no longer drain emotional energy through old negative reactions. The power of compassion will help you stay in your center, anchor insights along the way, and create new reference points from which you can make fresh choices.

From Mechanical Reaction to Compassionate Response

Jordan's continual mechanical reactions to the obstacles he met up with every day led to physical stress symptoms. Jordan felt that the pressure to get things done meant that he needed to push harder and faster to keep up. He describes feeling "an energy pressing against me as I moved through my day, like a wall of pressure inside my chest." Jordan isn't an isolated case. Millions of people feel "pressing energies" in their chest, head, or stomach. If not addressed, these pressures can lead to chest pains, headaches, gastric disorders, and other health problems.

When you feel something pressing against you, the mechanical response is to press back, to push harder to try to get through the resistance or clear the obstacle. But pressing back only creates rigidity and a fighting perspective. You can feel yourself rev up to overcome the resistance, or get dragged down by the weight of the situation. Either way, you get an uncomfortable feeling inside.

Instead of pushing against resistance, try relaxing to release the pressure. Learn to treat "pressing energies" as a warning signal that you're out of sync, out of a flow. Genuinely step back and relax while you slow your pace a bit. Ease back to your heart, breathe compassion and appreciation, and you will be surprised to find that you can often release the pressure and see an easier way through or around the obstacle. You'll get more done effectively, with less energy expenditure and fatigue.

The more you practice breathing compassion and befriending obstacles instead of resisting them, the better you'll be able to sustain a balanced rhythm and the more automatic your heart intuition will become. It's rhythm that empowers any new skill—riding a bike, playing golf, or learning to write—to become automatic. When children are learning to write, teachers have them practice the same letters over and over, to get the feel of the curve of the letters. All the practice pays off once the rhythm sets in. The teacher knows it's the rhythm of holding the pencil a certain way and practicing the curve that will help the student find a writing flow. Success is about sincerely practicing until the rhythm connects your heart (intuition), brain (memory), and nervous system (action).

The same is true with emotional skill. You learn to identify your emotional triggers, see what's underneath, and then get enough heart coherence going to manage your emotions through resistances that come up. Once you find your rhythm, it makes a huge difference in the enjoyment you can find in your work, the richness of your relationships, and the quality of your life.

Core Values

You increase your fulfillment in life as you act more from your core values. You can find out what your core values are by asking your heart what it would say, as you do in the Freeze-Frame technique. The heart often speaks simply, telling you to release, let go, forgive, move on. That's heart intelligence at work. If you look back at the exercises you've done in this book, you'll see that your heart's voice has core values of nonjudgment, appreciation, care, compassion, or forgiveness. Your heart knows that these core values create the foundation for effective and intelligent living.

Go back to chapters 6 and 7 and look at the answers your heart provided on your Freeze-Frame worksheet and Asset/Deficit Balance Sheet. Which of your core values did your heart suggest you use to turn deficits to assets? Did it urge you to forgive, let go, or ease up?

Scientific research backs up the importance of acting from your core values. A study on forgiveness at Stanford University showed that when people used the HeartMath tools, they experienced big reductions in feelings of anger. They found new ways to manage interpersonal hurts, and they became much more willing to use forgiveness as a problem-solving strategy (Luskin 1999). The core values of the heart will help you make better decisions and build your ability to stay in coherence.

Practicing the power of compassion will increase the effectiveness of all the heart tools and techniques you've learned. You will have more compassion for yourself and for others trying to manage or understand their emotions, especially in these rapidly changing times. Find core qualities in yourself and others that you value, and reinforce these values with the heart tools. Sincerely living from your core values at home and at work will keep your communications authentic and rapidly transform anger into compassionate understanding.

chapter 9

Transforming Anger at Home

If people could transform even 10 percent of the anger they experience at home, an untold number of divorces would be prevented. Anger—and the emotions that anger covers up—destroys relationships even when there is still heartfelt love. Anger erodes care and shuts down intuitive heart sensing. Anger in the home generates so much incoherence that it creates an atmosphere of fear, insecurity, and instability.

Research finds that one person's heart rhythm pattern can show up in another person's brain wave pattern when they are in close proximity. The electromagnetic energy generated by your heartbeat radiates outside your body. The rhythmic pattern of your heartbeat, which conveys your emotional state, is communicated electromagnetically to others (McCraty, Atkinson, et al. 1998). This means that your anger and incoherence can affect those close to you and their anger and incoherence can affect you.

Fortunately, a *coherent* heart rhythm can also affect those near to you. As you transform your anger, your increased coherence is communicated to those you love. They can feel the difference. They may not be able to put their finger on it, but they can sense more ease or harmony.

This electromagnetic communication is measurable (McCraty in press). It's not something mystical. It's physics. Harnessing the power of your heart rhythms is the power behind transformation.

Anne Berlin, a psychologist and certified HeartMath trainer with a private practice in La Jolla, California, uses HeartMath interventions with clients facing relationship challenges. Dr. Berlin finds that guiding couples in the Freeze-Frame technique can immediately reduce anger and hostility and greatly improve communication during the therapy session. She notes that in many cases, once one partner makes a positive emotional shift using the technique, it facilitates a shift on the part of the other partner as well. This profoundly improves communication between the two.

Dr. Berlin has also taught the Freeze-Frame technique to women experiencing difficulties in parenting. Some of these mothers were frustrated because they felt they had to keep repeating themselves in trying to communicate with and discipline their children. The women discovered that if they stopped and used Freeze-Frame when they found themselves in such a situation, the child would tend to respond to the mother's emotional shift and become more receptive to the mother's communication.

Michelle Baldwin is a licensed clinical social worker with a private practice in Chicago, Illinois, and is on the faculty of the Family Institute at Northwestern University and the Chicago Center for Family Health. She has found HeartMath techniques and tools particularly valuable in helping couples facing relationship distress. Dr. Baldwin has integrated the techniques both in her private practice and in a group program called PAIRS (Practical Application of Intimate Relationship Skills), a skills-based marriage education course geared toward relationship enhancement and divorce prevention, which she teaches with her husband, DeWitt

Baldwin, M.D., a psychiatrist and scholar-in-residence at the American Medical Association.

Dr. Baldwin found from her work with couples that the HeartMath interventions are especially valuable in facilitating better communication and improving anger management. In her experience, methods that encouraged the venting of angry feelings were not very helpful for clients. She reports, "HeartMath techniques are really the kind of skills people need when they are upset. They provide a much better and more mature way to handle negative feelings." She adds, "I also use the techniques and tools myself and consider them of tremendous value in mental health as an efficient method for therapists to regenerate and 'clear' themselves between clients."

What Triggers Your Anger at Home?

One of the best ways to start transforming anger in close relationships is to take an inventory of your common anger triggers when you're at home or with family members. Who or what causes you to react the most? Make a list, such as spouse, children, mother, paying bills, household chores, and so on.

Now, look for other situations where you commonly unload anger that could affect your family, and add those to your list. Are you prone to road rage? Do you get angry when your favorite team loses a game or an umpire makes a bad call? How about frustration from work that bleeds over into the home? Your family can become an easy outlet for venting leftover negative emotions from work.

Some deeper questions to pause and ask yourself: Do you get angry at people because you don't want to give up the sense of control over others that anger provides? Are you substituting intensity for intimacy? Is your anger a cover-up for feeling lonely, bored, restless, or empty? If you took away the feeling of anger, what would you find underneath?

Most anger expressed in the home is a cover-up for pain. You may feel clueless about the causes of your pain but you learned to get angry as a way to mask it. Remember that anger becomes a habit. If you get irritated at just the sound of your mother-in-law's voice on the phone, that's a mechanical reaction. After all, she hasn't said anything *yet* to trigger your anger.

Unresolved stress combined with a habitual response starts most anger reactions in the home. A habit is reinforced by repetition. Do you hear yourself saying over and over in your head, "If she (or he) would only _____, then _____"? When it comes to your kids, do you hear your head saying, "They keep doing _____, therefore I have a right to stay angry"? When your mind keeps recycling another person's faults, you get stuck in a loop of inner frustration. Anger keeps you on the attack, accusing others and feeling attacked and accused in return. The head defends with, "Yeah, but they _____," which keeps the anger going. You may have acquired this anger habit from parents or relatives while growing up.

Breaking the Cycle of Anger

To transform anger in the home, you have to break the cycle of anger. People go to marriage counselors, therapists, and ministers for help, but it often takes an external event to interrupt their anger pattern. Strong incoherent energy in families can continue for years, until eventually something erupts or breaks down and the pattern is disrupted. Too often, though, the pattern interrupter is separation or divorce, physical violence, jail, or a life-threatening illness.

You have the power to break the cycle before a catastrophe breaks it for you. The heart tools and techniques given in this book have been used with dramatic success to build coherence and transform the cycle of anger in situations that seemed hopeless.

Bob Rummel is a certified HeartMath coach who taught the techniques to members of a Native American tribe with a strong history of abuse. "The success stories," says Mr. Rummel, "are when people who were abused as children do not abuse their own kids. Through using HeartMath techniques, I've seen those cycles of abuse stopped dead in their tracks." One of the main techniques he teaches is Freeze-Frame. "The Freeze-Frame technique," he says, "is not a visualization or meditation. It's meant to be used in real life when someone's in your face, when you're considering what course of action to take." He adds, "The tool shifts you out of reactive thoughts. You Go to Neutral. It hooks you up to intuitive awareness."

Taking "Time-Out" to the Heart

One of the most common methods that people are taught for managing relationship anger is taking a time-out. Both partners agree to take a time-out if things get heated. They make a pact that if one calls a time-out, the other agrees to take a time-out too. They have hand signals to request a time-out if they can't get through the verbal barrage. What often happens, though, is one partner sincerely tries to take a time-out and the other goes along but hates it. Gary and Sue's story illustrates this problem.

"I'm usually the one who calls the time-out," says Sue. "Gary says he tries, but it doesn't work for him. Even if we stop talking, he's still fuming and his body language shows it." Gary is not able to change mood; it goes against the grain because his heart's not in it. Sue continues, "After I've managed to cool off, I end up blaming him for not really taking a time-out, thinking he doesn't care. Then I get angry again."

The fact is that Gary *can't* follow through without developing more of his own heart connection. Even if he tells himself to take a time-out, nothing shifts. Sue adds philosophically, "Sometimes I remember to tell myself that Gary's doing the best he can, so there's no point in getting mad. But it doesn't help me much. I still get angry that he won't take a real time-out."

To be effective, the time-out strategy has to be powered from the heart. Use the Freeze-Frame technique to transform your mental intention to take a time-out into a sincere heart action. Freeze-Frame will get your heart, brain, and nervous system in sync to add coherent power to your intention. You'll get in sync more quickly through learning to send heart energy of love and care to the other person. Go to your deeper heart, find a feeling of love or care, and radiate that caring energy. New perceptions will slip into your awareness right between the old head reactions of overcare, projection, judgment, blame, fear, or guilt. Several times a week, use the Heart Lock-In technique to radiate love and care into your home and to each other. It will cool your temper and show you a better way to respond. Then when you need to take a time-out in a moment of real anger, you will be able to slow-frame your mechanical reactions, recognize them as old head responses, and shift to the power of your heart to release them. A time-out in the heart – a time-out from your head reactions – is a real time-out.

If you use time-out as a discipline method with children, have them spend the time-out as a time-in the heart doing a Freeze-Frame. (If you've gotten upset or angry, give yourself a time-in the heart and do a Freeze-Frame as well.) If the child is old enough, ask her to write a Freeze-Frame worksheet and then show you what she wrote and talk about what her heart said. The discussion that follows about the difference between her head reaction and her heart's perspective can be very productive.

Through radiating love, care, and compassion from the heart, you can respect your differences with your partner or children and still stay in your own center. The process of shifting intention to the heart and radiating love or care enables the power of the heart to work for you, often resulting in new insights for dealing with issues. A little appreciation or compassion can go a long way to increase coherence in a home. Your partner and children have personalities different from yours. They perceive differently. One person's way of looking at things isn't better or worse. It's just that some personalities are more challenged in managing emotions. It's through the heart that even those who are challenged most can begin to see new options for emotional control.

Authentic Communication

The headline on *CNN.com* read, "Housewife Seeking Appreciation Quits Housework" (Associated Press 2002). Fed up with the responsibility of working, going to school, and doing all the household chores while her husband went fishing, the woman went on strike. She refused to do the laundry, cook, or make the bed. Somehow the local newspaper picked it up, and soon she was asked to be on local TV, *Inside Edition,* and *Good Morning America.* Calls poured in from around the world. The woman reminded interviewers that she wasn't looking for publicity; it was a personal campaign for some appreciation. According to the woman, her husband was amazed and perhaps a little shocked by it all.

Amusing as it seems, this woman's story struck a chord in thousands of women who feel unappreciated, taken for granted, and unable to communicate their needs to their spouses. Of course we're not suggesting that you go on strike in an effort to communicate, but it is important for your health and well-being that you learn how to authentically communicate your needs.

Studies have shown that while marital discord causes emotional pain to both partners, a woman's cardiovascular health may be especially vulnerable to the effects of anger. According to one study, women who admitted an inability to regulate their anger were not only less satisfied with their marriage, they were also less able to apply the physiological "brake pedal" — the parasympathetic nervous system — to slow their heartbeat and make it less strong, thereby calming themselves. "All they have is a gas pedal," says Dr. Sybil Carrère, the study's investigator, referring to the sympathetic nervous system, "not a brake pedal" (Huggins 2002). This type of physiological response may be associated with heart disease and other health problems.

Using the heart tools, you can apply your brake pedal (the parasympathetic nervous system) and slow your heart down. You can also use the tools to find ways to authentically communicate. Authentic communication starts with listening to your own heart. Head reactions like judgment, blame, resentment, and overcare cause a traffic jam between your heart and the higher perceptual centers in your brain. So when you try to listen, all that inner noise creates a mental filter. Using the Freeze-Frame technique during communication helps eliminate the static so you can hear your heart and communicate effectively.

Start with a Freeze-Frame worksheet to help you gain clarity about what your heart intuition has to say. On a piece of paper, write down the relationship or communication issue. Next, write down your head reactions regarding the issue: thoughts, emotional responses, your inner dialogue with yourself about it, and what you have been doing to address the issue. Then go through the steps of the Freeze-Frame technique. Be open and vulnerable to your heart feelings and ask for a new perspective. When you're done, write down your heart perceptions and any intuitive ideas for solutions.

Relationships would flourish if families felt safe to share their heart feelings and perceptions. Because heart feelings are sensitive, safety requires listening to each other from a place of neutral in the heart. Use Go to Neutral and

Freeze-Frame to enable yourself to listen with an open heart until the person is finished speaking or until there is a natural pause in the conversation. Then you can respond from your own heart feelings. We call this process *Intuitive Listening*. If your partner agrees, try the Intuitive Listening exercise together.

Communication exercises need to come from the heart to be most effective, with both partners practicing heart vulnerability. When you are the speaker, being heart vulnerable means listening to your own heart and sincerely communicating what you feel. When you are the listener, being heart vulnerable means listening to another person's heart without your mind filtering what it wants or projecting a motive onto the other person.

🖉 *Intuitive Listening*

1. *Freeze-Frame for thirty seconds to gain clarity about what you want to say. Decide who will share first. It's important that the sharing not be longer than one minute.*

2. *Freeze-Frame and stay neutral while your partner is sharing for one minute. Feeling appreciation for your partner will help you stay focused in the heart, and help your partner feel more secure.*

3. *Say back, in your own words, the essence of what you heard.*

4. *Fine-tune for accuracy before you add your own comments and insights. Ask your partner if he or she felt heard and understood. If not, repeat steps 2 and 3.*

5. *Switch roles.*

Many communication workshops teach a method called *active listening*, which involves mirroring or feeding back what the other person has said to check for accuracy. If done just with the head memorizing the words, it comes across as insincere parroting. Much of the feeling and essence is lost. When you add the heart to active listening, you hear the other person's essence and real meaning, *even if their words are saying something different.* Active listening turns into Intuitive Listening, and the other person feels heard and understood.

Make Intuitive Listening a new habit. You can use it whether or not the other person does. With just a little practice, you will find yourself automatically shifting to the heart and listening from neutral. The more coherence you bring to relationship interactions, the richer they become.

Intuitive Listening with Children

Children shape their values as they hear family members share feelings and views, and observe how adults deal with challenges. If you are unable to manage your emotions or your anger, your children will most likely learn those emotional behaviors from you. However, if you show that you are making efforts to handle and resolve your emotions, you can help your children better manage theirs.

Intuitive Listening helps children feel more secure in sharing. It also helps them more honestly communicate their feelings of anger, fear, or guilt and learn to respect and have compassion for others' feelings. Andrew, age fourteen, says, "It showed me a lot about self-control, the emotions, and all of that. It's a great concept, how you can just stop and then think about what you're gonna say—think with your heart instead of your mind—and do it more peacefully."

At family meetings, take turns doing the Intuitive Listening exercise until everyone has had a chance to be speaker and listener with everyone else in the family. You can do this over a period of days. Other family members who are observing can use Freeze-Frame and send out love and appreciation to the two practicing. Send out care and compassion if they're having a hard time. After everyone has tried it, remind each other to use Intuitive

Listening during casual conversations. When people start inter-rupting or talking over each other, call a time-out and remind everyone to listen from the heart.

As a family, talk about what adds to or takes away from coherence and bonding in your family. Together, do an Asset/Defi-cit Balance Sheet about your family. As sensitive issues are dis-cussed, use the Intuitive Listening exercise. Talk about the heart tools and how to use them. Discuss which tools each person could use to help increase the assets and reduce the deficits. Talk about how you are using the tools and in what ways they are helping you. Keep a family journal of everyone's progress. These family activities don't have to take a lot of time, and they can be incredibly powerful in transforming the anger in a home.

Raymundo, age sixteen, introduced the heart tools and Intuitive Listening to his family after learning them in his classroom. He says, "I learned how to use the heart and brain together to become a better person and to understand what the other person is talking about—to communicate more instead of having all the anger inside you. It is good!"

chapter 10

Transforming Anger in the Workplace

The people who make up a home or a workplace set the emotional tone or attitude for that environment. In the workplace, this is referred to as the *organizational climate*. When employees invest a significant amount of energy in negative emotional processes, their ability to relate diminishes, their energy drains more quickly, productivity is hampered, and their enjoyment of work is reduced. Emotional incoherence affects the entire company.

Mergers, acquisitions, and downsizings are often coupled with lack of care, leaving workers with a buildup of unresolved judgments, blame, and anger. While short-term profits might go up, the negative undercurrent of emotional drain, low morale, and subterfuge never gets accounted for on balance sheets and is often more costly in the long term than companies understand. A 1999 study on anger in the workplace shows that one in four employees admits to being "generally or at least somewhat angry" at work (Girardet). The reasons include increasing workloads, the actions of supervisors or managers, and a lack of appreciation. Since then, the stress produced by these issues has become even more intense. Almost monthly, new studies are showing that workplace stress continues to skyrocket. One study by the National Institute for Occupational Safety and Health reported that more than half of all employees in the U.S. feel work stress is a major issue in their lives, while 42 percent feel others in their company need help managing their stress (Daniels 2002).

From the executive suite to the shop floor, admitting you are stressed out is often taboo. You're supposed to be working longer and harder. "In an environment where you think people are satisfied with their jobs, there is a sort of undercurrent of anger and resentment aimed at the workplace," says Donald Gibson, a professor at the Yale University School of Management (Girardet 1999). Anger at work generally comes from feeling that you or others are being treated unfairly and from a sense that you're helpless to do anything about it.

Lack of emotional management skills and high stress are behind rising incidences of work-related violence. The increase in rage has spawned new terms including *techno rage* (abuse of office equipment that won't work well or fast enough), *desk rage* (screaming at customers or coworkers or just at one's own workload), and *road rage* (outbursts of aggression while driving). Yet Gibson's 1999 study found that most effects of workplace anger are more subtle. They include a hostile work environment and the tendency to do the minimum amount of work necessary to get by. In 1995, it was estimated that work stress costs employers more than $200 billion a year in lost productivity, absenteeism, and increased health-care costs, and that number has skyrocketed to over $300 billion since then (National Safety Council).

James K. Clifton, chairman and chief executive officer of Gallup, known for its national polls, understands that emotions are a critical factor in business success. In his 2002 article, "Winning Business in the Emotional Economy," he cites statistics showing that organizations achieve sustainable growth not with accounting schemes but by harnessing the unwieldy power of human emotions. Clifton writes, "The success of your organization doesn't depend on your understanding of economics, or organizational development, or marketing. It depends, quite simply, on your understanding of psychology: how each individual employee connects with your customers; how each individual employee connects with your company."

Workplace stress and anger have a cascade effect on family and society. In a survey of American working mothers, 70 percent say they most frequently take workplace stress out on their spouses, and that a strained relationship with their spouse or children represents the largest intangible toll of job stress (Rosch 1997). Stella, an accountant and mother of two, told us in a HeartMath seminar,

> *Since the downsizing, I'm constantly under time*
> *pressures at work and have to take work home. I feel*
> *guilty I can't help my kids with their homework and*
> *barely have time to get housework done. I'm irritable*
> *and angry because I see no way out.*

A startling 80 percent of drivers in the U.S. admit they are angry most or all of the time while driving (Ferguson 1998). Their most common reason is lack of time, or simply running late. According to the U.S. Department of Transportation, road rage contributes to one-third of traffic accidents involving injury and two-thirds of those that result in death.

High stress at work is also a factor in the current epidemic of obesity in the U.S. Frayed nerves increase the desire for carbohydrates and fat. And if the pressure is chronic, the body tries even harder to hold on to the pounds. Looking and feeling fat only adds to most people's self-directed anger. Suppressed anger in the workplace can lead to negative health outcomes, such as anxiety, depression, high blood pressure, and heart disease. A 2002 study published in the

British Medical Journal found that "healthy people with stressful jobs who work long hours but get little satisfaction from what they do have twice the risk of dying from heart disease as satisfied employees . . . even after controlling for the effects of conventional cardiovascular risk factors" (Reaney). Women are much less likely than men to express their anger, but anger in women also goes straight to the heart. In a long-range study, middle-aged women who swallow their anger and often worry about making a good impression showed biological signs that point to an increased risk of heart attack before age sixty (Matthews et al. 1998). Other studies show that for women and men who have had a heart attack, acute episodes of anger during emotional conflict more than double the risk of another heart attack in the subsequent two hours (Mittleman et al. 1995). And in those with coronary artery disease, just *recalling* a feeling of anger is more potent than other mental stressors or even physical exercise in constricting blood flow (Ironson et al. 1992).

Developing Business Heart

Think of all the people interacting under one roof at work. There are so many complex individual and interpersonal psychologies involved, and when you add the pressures of today's work challenges, it's no wonder the workplace is a pressure cooker. The only thing that will improve a stressful organizational climate is more care and more heart. You can't have a coherent organization without heart. It seems counterintuitive to many that adding heart will improve the bottom line. Some people still think that a only a hard-driving head will increase profitability. The heart is still seen as soft and squishy, too emotional. And many supervisors don't know how to deal with their own emotions, let alone guide others. So emotions get swept aside and productivity is lost because the emotional climate is not addressed.

But some companies are beginning to realize you need both a strong head and a strong heart to succeed. They understand there is a link between emotions and performance. They know the old saying "Leave your emotions at the door when you come to work" is outdated. To improve performance and customer service, they are trying to increase heart qualities of appreciation and care. They are looking for what we call *business heart* – a practical, measurable, and replicable approach to resolving emotional stress at work.

World-class companies like Sony, Shell, Cisco, Boeing, Unilever, and BP are providing HeartMath training to executives and employees. Results have been dramatic in giving employees emotional self-management skills as well as improving organizational climate, job satisfaction, productivity, and health. After HeartMath's "Power to Change Performance" training, employees ranging from executives to front-line workers were able to significantly decrease their anger, depression, and anxiety; find relief from stress symptoms such as fatigue, body aches, and stomach problems; and sustain those improvements long after the training ended (Barrios-Choplin, McCraty, and Atkinson 1999). In one Fortune 100 information technology company, pre- and post-training surveys showed that the percentage of employees who frequently experienced anger was reduced from 42 percent to 9 percent after three months. Surveys of nearly 1,400 employees at six global companies showed the following pooled results after six months: 60 percent reduction in anxiety, 45 percent reduction in exhaustion, 41 percent reduction in intent to leave the job, 24 percent improvement in ability to focus, 25 percent improvement in listening ability, and 17 percent reduction in home-work conflict. Employees used the HeartMath tools and techniques in the workplace, at home, on the road—everywhere. One senior executive said, "This isn't just stress management; it's stress transformation."

The financial return to companies has also been significant. Delnor Hospital, near Chicago, used HeartMath's training and Freeze-Framer heart rhythm feedback software (see chapter 11) in the hopes of reducing staff turnover, and then measured the financial impact. Employee turnover dropped from 28 percent to 20.9 percent in one year among the entire staff of one thousand, but decreased to just 5.7 percent for the four hundred staff members who received HeartMath training. This represented an annualized savings of $800,000 for the hospital. Medicare patients' average length of stay in the hospital decreased by 9 percent, which management attributed to reduced staff stress and improved performance and care. This represented another $1.4 million in annualized savings. Delnor was awarded the prestigious Corporate Health and Productivity Management Award in 2002 for demonstrating the relationship between health and productivity by initiating intervention and measuring the resulting changes.

A climate of increased organizational coherence is palpable. You can feel it. People move in a balanced and upbeat rhythm with care and warmth. They have the clarity to see what needs to be done and the flexibility to meet challenges and react to emergencies, as a hospital must be able to do at any moment. While your company leadership may still ignore emotional issues, you can't afford this approach and you don't have to. If you're like most people, you spend most of your waking hours at work. The feelings and attitudes you experience there count. To protect your heart and your health, you need to transform your anger at work. Your increased coherence will begin to change your work environment. You can start by using the tools and techniques you've learned in this book to put out more heart. You don't have to be perfect at it. Even a little bit of heart goes a long way.

Do an Asset/Deficit Balance Sheet (from chapter 7) on your workplace assets and deficits. Do it as an exercise in self-care. Write down the tools you could use to increase the assets and reduce the deficits, and then use them. Where could you Go to Neutral more and drain less of your energy? Where could you add some appreciation? How could you stop contributing to an environment of incoherence? Acting on your answers is showing deeper care for yourself and others. Listen to your heart intuition even if nothing around you seems to change. Doing so will help draw new opportunities to you, give you confidence to make a needed job change, or allow you to make peace with what you can't change. You don't have to stay resigned to a negative work environment. Others have found a new rhythm at work using the tools; so can you.

Finding Your Rhythm under Pressure

Use Go to Neutral when you feel tension and pressure. Find neutral to release judgments and blame, then add Attitude Breathing of compassion and care for yourself. This will help shift your perceptions of and reactions to time pressures. Jodi describes how this works for her:

> In the past months I've been hit with a bigger workload. On top of my regular job, there have been many unexpected and unplanned-for things coming across my desk, all of them needing to be addressed now. When I tackle them from my mind, I see no way to get them all done in time. My mind projects I'll be working until midnight or something will fall through the cracks. Then I start judging people in my way and get real angry. I've found that by using Go to Neutral I create breathing space. My brain shifts. I see from a different view, and time shifts. Everything

> *gets done, and I often have time to spare. I find I*
> *have to hold on to neutral in the heart, because if I go*
> *back to my mind I start projecting the worst again.*

You will become time-efficient in new ways as you get your heart and brain more in sync. Your heart intelligence will show you what's important and what's not. The real priorities will get done. *If you start feeling overwhelmed, just go to neutral nonjudgment and do Attitude Breathing to get back in sync.* In those times when you really can't get everything done, Going to Neutral will show you how to address it, either by communicating with a superior or by flexing and working the extra time, without draining your energy in frustration or anger.

Donna explains,

> *I don't know how many times simply telling myself to*
> *Go to Neutral in the heart and breathing compassion*
> *for myself through the heart and solar plexus has*
> *saved me from blowing up. It's simple, but it does*
> *change my perspective so I feel in control and I make*
> *better decisions from there. My boss really respects the*
> *changes he's seen in me.*

Finding Your Rhythm in Communication Issues

Most workplace anger results from unresolved communication issues. You can waste a lot of energy and time working yourself into a tizzy, thinking or talking about who said what or what unfair policy came down. Managers who can't manage their emotions leave a wake of incoherence as they change decisions, bark orders, or fail to communicate. The emotional negativity casts a pall over the entire workplace.

Underneath anger is always a pile-up of judgment, blame, and projection, which creates fear and tension. You may find yourself generalizing about what the problem is and who's responsible. One loaded word, like *them, they, him, her,* or *that,* says it all. "They" — usually company management — are doing it to me. "He" or "she" doesn't care how hard I'm working. "They" don't treat us fairly. When Pat critiqued an employee in a performance review, she was met with a barrage of one-word blames. "They" were all wrong, "that" was unfair, coworkers were stupid and always getting in the way. Pat had the employee explain each accusation, and they all boiled down to two situations in which there had been a lack of clear communication. While there are plenty of uncaring company policies and uncaring supervisors and coworkers, unresolved anger is still your emotional responsibility. You are the one who victimizes yourself most. Blaming "her" or "them" is deflecting responsibility for your own energy and health. Unresolved anger causes a sense of entitlement, and you forget that you are the one who has to make it better inside yourself first.

Some companies provide communications skills training, but these skills are usually not enough. To communicate effectively, you have to first manage your emotional reactions. You can't just say "I need to be more assertive," then march into your supervisor's office, make demands, and expect those demands to be met. *Instead, try writing out the facts, then determine a fair request, and write down consequences you can live with. Use a Freeze-Frame worksheet to help you determine what's "fair" from the heart. Then decide if you still want to speak up. The next step is to find your rhythm. Use the Freeze-Frame technique again to find a heart-intuitive perspective on how best to communicate. When you present your concern or request, utilize the Intuitive Listening exercise in chapter 9. No one needs to know you are doing it. You will be able to intuitively tune in to the essence and subtle nuances of what the other person*

*is saying and not react to his or her words or emotions. Use the
Freeze-Frame technique to authentically communicate – to listen
from the heart and speak your truth from the heart.*

- *Freeze-Frame to get clarity about what you want to say.*

- *Freeze-Frame and remain neutral as you listen.*

- *Freeze-Frame your head chatter.*

- *Freeze-Frame and add outgoing care, appreciation, or
  compassion as you speak.*

Assertiveness without *care* will block intuitive connection with the other person. Some people care naturally, so learning to speak from the heart is easier for them. Other people have a strong mind or intellect, so asserting from the mind is easier. They hold their own, but often by asserting an unreasonable position without enough give and take. They may get their way, but at the expense of meaningful dialogue. Communicating from the mind without enough heart will only come across as posturing. Too often, assertiveness training encourages people to blurt out the first thing that comes to mind, which may be blame and anger. This only alienates the other person and cuts off the communication.

When you add the heart, assertiveness becomes easier and more effective. This new kind of assertiveness training is an inside job at first. You assert heart vulnerability to yourself, listening to your heart to learn what needs to be said. Then you speak from your heart with care but without overcare. You can get your point across without being threatening, and hold your center even if the other person reacts. *This is business heart.* Use Go to Neutral, and send out genuine care no matter what comes up. You'll build heart power and sensitivity, which allows you to connect with others on a deeper level.

You'll need heart power to stay centered during a difficult communication. Heart power will show you how to stand up for your needs. Being heart vulnerable does not mean allowing others to walk all over you. Heart power will show you how to respond appropriately without anger or blame. Heart power builds a business heart of care and clarity. Michael Maccoby, director of the Harvard Project on Technology, Work, and Character, writes that "The heart is a symbol for knowledge, purpose, courage. It is a muscle, just like any other muscle, and it has to be exercised to become a strong heart ... One has to dedicate oneself to develop the heart, just as one develops the head" (Maccoby 1976).

As you learn to communicate from a deep heart, you will be able to observe your mind and emotions rather than just react to them. You can watch your mental and emotional triggers start to go off, then Go to Neutral instead of acting on them. Deep heart is simply a deeper, more authentic intent that generates more coherence, more power. And it empowers you to give out what you want—real care, nonjudgment, appreciation, compassion—and find yourself getting more of it in return.

Learning to be solidly heart assertive does not always imply speaking out more. If you're someone who feels it would be easier to walk in front of a truck than to speak about what's bothering you, simply be more assertive about sending out love and care. You can shift to a genuine *attitude* of care even when you feel resistance inside or can't find a *feeling* of care. Listen to your heart, and you will intuitively sense the appropriate way to connect with another person. It may be writing a note, or inviting someone to lunch to get to know each other better, or something else that feels intuitively right.

To communicate is to connect so the other person gets your care and your real intent. Intuition can direct you in being authentic so that what you say has a higher chance of connecting with the other person's heart if he or she is open. Of course, you can't make someone hear you. But you can care enough to try, and stay solid in your heart even if they don't hear you. You can learn to communicate—to get it out—but from the heart. You will no longer feel like you have to resign yourself to a negative situation, since you can assertively listen to and follow your heart intuition. Just doing that will be a relief.

To practice this new type of heart assertiveness, do a Freeze-Frame worksheet (see chapter 6) on a recent work-related issue that provoked anger and is still causing you stress. Then, with care and courage, act on the intuitive perspective you get.

Emotional histories will always be acted out in the workplace, and anger and its underlying emotions will always be triggered—that's the nature of life. But you can transform your negative feelings with inner technologies so *you* aren't continually triggered and drained. This transformation happens in steps. It starts with managing your reactions with business heart. Then with each new situation you bring work pressures and communication issues under your control in a new way.

Roger's Story

Roger is a manager who struggled with anger management for thirty years. Roger's symptoms included hair-trigger reactions and combative or belligerent responses. However, Roger was also known for his patience, kindness, and caring. You just never knew which Roger you were going to get. Although his supervisors had warned him over the years to control his anger, Roger felt that his anger was something others wanted him to change so they could get the better of him. After some counseling, he gave his direct reports permission to point out his reactivity. He wanted to learn how not to get defensive or justify himself when he did. It was a struggle, because Roger often did not agree that he was being reactive and would stay on the offensive. This, of course, did not encourage his team members to keep pointing out his reactivity.

Roger's change came after he learned the heart tools.

I have taught myself through practice of the tools to slow-frame what happens inside me. I trigger when I feel attacked, then I have highly derogatory thoughts toward the offender. Now I can catch it when those thoughts arise. Before the second thought forms, I tell myself to Freeze-Frame and come to balance before responding. I can see that this is triggering a change in my brain, because soon I'm having intuitive thoughts of understanding why the person is behaving that way. I can see the person is upset, but it's not an attack on me personally. So I can reply with compassion.

Roger wrote us that his greatest reward is the knowledge that he can manage his strong emotional reactions, and a bonus is the look on the face of the person who did not expect a kind reply from him. Roger says he still needs to remain alert, especially when he feels misjudged or treated unfairly. "I use the tool Go to Neutral a lot, to gain a different perspective on the situation and release the hurt/angry reaction before it governs my next action. I also have to stay diligent not to build expectations of how others should behave toward me, especially in situations where I feel I have been caring for them over a long period of time, because I can have a nasty blow-up."

Roger has found that using the heart tools in his workplace has spilled over into other parts of his life. "I was your typical road-rage maniac," Roger admits.

A situation happened last week that would have ended up totally different not long ago. I was driving to work on a narrow uphill street that I don't ordinarily take and got stuck behind an old VW bug

*going fifteen miles an hour. At first I was
philosophical, thinking that those old bugs couldn't go
any faster. When the road widened a bit, I tried to
pass the guy and he sped up and wouldn't let me. I
started to get ticked off and tailgated him the five
remaining blocks to work. When I pulled into the
parking lot, he drove up beside me screaming, "Don't
you know that road has a fifteen-mile-an-hour limit?"
I was taken aback but did a quick Freeze-Frame and
asked, "Is the whole road fifteen miles an hour?" He
softened a little and answered, "No, some of it is
twenty-five." Then he quickly got angry again, yelling
"Want to make something out of it? Want to get out
of the car and fight?" My trigger reaction was,
"Yeah — let's do it," then I thought, we're right
outside the company offices, so I did Freeze-Frame to
ask my heart what to say now that wouldn't
exacerbate the problem. I told him, "I really don't
want to get angry and don't want to do anything to
upset you more. In today's world I don't want to add
more negativity to the atmosphere we all have to live
in." As I spoke I felt a level of peace, and I added,
"You know, I want to apologize for anything I may
have done as we went up the road that may have
caused any disturbance in you." His whole body
softened and relaxed, and he drove away.*

chapter 11

It's All about Heart

Transforming Anger is all about redirecting your power. You use the power of your heart to bring about a transformation in your emotional habits. Your heart draws on a different source of power—your own real spirit—to bring about change. As many cultures, religions, and spiritual traditions throughout human history have known, the heart is a gateway to one's higher self or spirit—a source of love, of wisdom, and of power.

Love and its ingredients, such as care, appreciation, compassion, and forgiveness, have long been associated with transformation. These heartfelt positive emotions create a physiological state of heart rhythm coherence, which gives you more power to make the changes you want to see in yourself. Activating the power of your heart is not an overnight fix for rage, anger, or frustration, but it empowers you to do things you haven't been able to do consistently—or at all.

People entering coherent heart rhythm states frequently report feelings of increased spiritual connection. Heart rhythm coherence creates alignment with your real spirit. You may find that as you use the heart tools and techniques in this book, your heart opens to new spiritual awareness.

Depending on your particular belief system, you might feel a greater connection to God, more unity with others, or freer access to an intuitive intelligence or a higher aspect of yourself. Some people describe experiencing an inner quiet along with deep feelings of security, peace, and love.

Here is one person's experience of regularly practicing the heart tools: "You feel a deep sense of peace and internal balance—you are at harmony with yourself, with others, and with your larger environment. You experience increased buoyancy, vitality, and flow. Your senses are enlivened—your perceptual experience seems richer, more textured. Intuitive insight suddenly provides convenient solutions to problems that had previously consumed weeks of restless thought. Your creativity flows freely."

For most people, moments of heightened spiritual awareness are rare and occur unpredictably, rather than being intentionally self-generated. A main reason for this is a lack of mental and emotional self-management skills. In essence, the "inner noise" and incoherence generated by mental and emotional turbulence prevent people from feeling genuine, positive emotions more consistently and sustaining states of enhanced spiritual connection. It's time for people on the planet to learn about the ingredients of love and their power to facilitate change.

The Care Shift

The world is moving at breakneck speed, which speeds up people's anger reactions. Everywhere we look we see incoherence and chaos. Information is moving faster, and much of it is disturbing news. But out of personal and social incoherence comes new opportunity. Out of chaos comes order. People are going back to their hearts to find new values. There is a *care shift* going on underneath the emotional chaos.

J. Walter Smith, President of Yankelovich, Inc., describes this shift in a 2002 Yankelovich Monitor national survey. He finds that Americans are putting more emphasis on values and yearning for them. Many have lost faith in politics, the financial markets, and organized religion. Scandals have eroded confidence in traditional institutions. People are redefining what's important. There's an emerging shift toward family, connectivity, balance, integrity, authenticity, and spirituality.

We call this a care shift because people are really yearning for the core values of the heart. They are searching for the missing ingredients of love and deeper care. These qualities are available within the heart of each person. It's *really wanting them* that opens them up. Deeper care opens the heart to intuitive insight. As the heart opens, more of your real spirit or higher self integrates with your human nature and gets expressed in interactions with others. The core values of the heart can't just be philosophized, assumed, or pontificated. They have to be *actualized* in human consciousness. To care deeply is to actualize love rather than just assume you love.

The fast pace of modern life intensifies mental and emotional ups and downs. Most people want to feel better more of the time. It takes love in action, or deeper care, to feel better. The heart tool of sending love and compassion to yourself, while in the midst of an anger trigger or a surfacing emotional history, is powerful care in action. Care gives you an emotional *choice* to go the old way or a new way from your heart intelligence. Anger, like a drug, can feel good in the moment, but the consequences are painful, unless you just go numb in the energy drain that follows.

Despite people's best intentions, human nature has a "negativity bias"—a tendency to focus more on negative thoughts and emotions than on positive or even neutral ones. This is a very real phenomenon with a sound neurophysiological basis (Ito et al. 1998). Although most people claim that of course they love, they care, they appreciate, it might shock them to realize the large degree to which they are merely acknowledging or assuming these feelings, rather than truly feeling or experiencing them. Many people don't realize the extent to which negative emotional patterns dominate their internal landscape, the negativity having become so familiar and ingrained that it seems to be part of their identity. These ongoing negative feelings and thoughts drain vital energy from their emotional reserves, which need to be replenished to sustain positive emotional and spiritual experiences.

Spiritual hope is knowing you can change the emotional habits and neural patterns holding you back. You can rewire your brain for transformation. Recent research has overturned old beliefs that brain circuits in adults cannot be changed. It is now recognized that the brain is able to forge new connections among its neurons and rewire itself. Neuroscientists have found that the regions of the brain that get the most use literally expand (Schwartz and Begley 2002a). For example, people who play the violin get more neurons assigned to the fingers of their left hand, which play the strings, than people who don't use their left hand as much. Even if you take up the violin at age forty, with regular practice you will still generate this brain reorganization. And practice doesn't have to be physical. Mental rehearsal causes just as large a change. Those in the same study who were asked to rehearse by merely thinking about moving their left fingers produced brain changes comparable to those generated by violinists actually moving their fingers (Elbert et al. 1995).

This study has tremendous implications. It means that whatever you focus on and repeat—whether negative thoughts and anger reactions or positive emotions—will increase the amount of brain territory devoted to those activities. In other words, whatever you practice, the brain reinforces. An article reporting on this research concludes, "The brain is dynamic, and the life we lead leaves its mark in the complex circuitry of the brain—footprints of the experiences we have had, the thoughts we have thought, the actions we have taken. The brain allocates neural real estate depending on what we use most. . . . But the brain also remakes itself based on something much more ephemeral than what we do: It rewires itself based on what we think" (Schwartz and Begley 2002b). Our research and experience with the heart tools suggests that what we feel is more powerful than what we think in transforming neural patterns. This is because feeling underlies and motivates thought.

The Earth is a planet of feeling as well as thought. A planet of heart as well as mind. Transforming emotional histories and anger is the next stage of human evolution, and it is essential for planetary survival. Transforming destructive emotions requires the power of the heart. So techniques that connect you with your deeper heart are the key. Increasing your heart rhythm coherence connects you with your inner source of power and intuition. It synchronizes your heart and brain so you can receive more downloads of intuitive information from your spirit, your deeper intelligence. Coherence (love) is a scientifically based, universal guiding principle for human behavior. Coherence provides a new paradigm for psychology.

It's Heart Time

The heart has been ignored, misunderstood, or swept under the carpet in much of modern psychology. The focus has been on the brain and mind as the sole determinants of behavior. Now that the link between emotions and the heart has been scientifically established, it's time to bring back the heart. Emotional transformation and spiritual enlightenment will not happen—and cannot be sustained—without the heart. The mind alone can't keep up with the speed of changes happening in the world. You need intuitive heart feeling to sense appropriate directions for you and those you care about.

As the pace of change continues to accelerate, it will require you to *act faster* on your heart's promptings to let go of rage, frustration, and irritation and to release emotional histories. Otherwise, the negative emotional telepathy of others and the pull from a negative environment can increase your own negativity. Remember that none of your emotional "stuff" that comes up is bad. *It has to come up to be transformed.* You now have the tools you need to transform it. Realize that the heart tools give you the power to choose a new way and not go down the same predictable path. In these times of accelerated change, your spirit is bringing up old issues for you to take to heart and transform – not to work over again and again. From your heart you'll see, in real time, that rage or frustration is a choice. You will be able to slow-frame and see that you can choose the mechanical anger reaction, or you can choose Go to Neutral and ease. Both options will be there. The more you shift to the power of your heart and choose ease, the more you strengthen the connection between your spirit and your humanness. While choosing the heart can feel awkward at times, eventually going the way of anger will feel more awkward to you.

You will start to see changes in yourself as soon as you begin practicing the HeartMath tools and techniques. Thousands have used these tools successfully at home, at work, and at school. People are often surprised at how quickly they see results. It's heart time. Spend time in the heart and develop your emotional skills.

You will accelerate your progress if you do the written exercises in this book and periodically go back and read what you have written. If you get stuck, ask your heart honestly, "What are the things that are holding me back?" Use an Asset/Deficit Balance Sheet or a Freeze-Frame worksheet, and you will get answers.

If there's a lot of negativity in your environment, in your home or workplace, you'll need a new level of sincere heart intention to offset its effects or make a needed change. Go to Neutral, Attitude Breathing, Freeze-Frame, and Intuitive Listening are all effective tools for protecting yourself and helping transform the negativity around you. Using them will bring you more quality and happiness in your interactions with others. It won't be long before using the tools will become automatic as they become programmed in your neural circuits. Your heart intuition will flow in more easily and remind you which tools to use and when.

Below are specific tips that can help.

Setting Up Your Day: The Thirty-Minute Game. *Starting your day right in the heart can make a big difference in your power to transform negative emotions the rest of the day. You can give yourself a jump-start in the heart each morning by playing what we call "the thirty-minute game."*

As soon as you wake up in the morning, go to your heart and start Attitude Breathing. Breathe love or appreciation through your heart for a full minute. When you get out of bed, take the first thirty minutes of your day to anchor those attitudes in your heart by continuing to breathe love or appreciation through the heart and solar plexus while you're moving around doing morning activities. If you can't feel anything positive or are having a hard time with yourself, your spouse, or your kids, then breathe compassion instead. Have the integrity to activate the power of compassion no matter what's going on inside you or around you. Be sincere and genuine in your efforts to play the thirty-minute game, and you will find it easier to stay emotionally centered in a balanced attitude throughout the day. You will be setting up a heart reference point right at the start of your day that you can return to at any time.

Modulation. *There will be hours or days when you will experience periods of modulation. One moment you feel appreciation or*

*joy, and the next you feel anger, irritation, or resistance. Or sud-
denly you feel emotionally empty, dry, or flat. This doesn't always
mean there's something wrong or that you blew it. Emotional energies, at times, readjust in the human system, and this is happening
to people in more extreme ways during this time of global change.
It's what you do with the emotional fluctuations that matters. As
soon as you sense that you're out of sync, grab a heart tool and use
it. Don't overpersonalize an emotional fluctuation by feeling you
did something bad. That will only prolong the modulation. You can
ride through periods of modulation with more balance if you make a
deeper effort to connect with your heart and put out more care
when your attitude starts to fade.*

Being Earnest. *Make care for your heart your first priority. It
takes commitment to put your heart first. You'll find that commitment not because you "should," but because of your own intelligence. Your own commonsense wisdom will tell you that your heart
is where you will find more fulfillment in life.*

*Honoring your commitment to your heart is not about never
getting angry again, because you will. It's about how earnestly you
choose the heart and Go to Neutral or use Attitude Breathing or
Freeze-Frame. Think of your emotions and actions as bound by a
rubber band that only goes so far out before you pull yourself back
to the heart. Being committed means pulling back from emotional
reactions before the rubber band stretches too far and painfully
snaps back on you. Using a tool isn't about doing it perfectly; it's
about being "onto yourself" – understanding how anger cascades in
you and making a sincere effort to go back to the heart.*

*Be earnest in doing the Heart Lock-In technique so you build
stronger ability to stay in your heart. You will learn to distinguish
more subtly between your head and heart voices. You will also
develop your skill at directing or sending heart energy of love,
appreciation, care, or compassion to other people. Then when negative situations happen, you'll be able to send heart energy – not so
another person will change, but to build your own cushion of
response to people and situations so they don't get to you as much.*

Use the Intuitive Listening exercise to learn to hear others' hearts, not just their words. Learn to be heart assertive and communicate your truth with authenticity. This will help you protect yourself from other people's emotional baggage and can help to transform an environment of negativity.

Making Peace with "What Is." Finding more fulfillment in life means learning how to creatively change what you can change and make peace with the things you can't. This can be especially hard if you are someone who gets impatient over small inconveniences or if behind your anger or frustration lies a strong sense of entitlement, a belief that life "owes" you. This will keep you in turmoil. Making peace with "what is" is a powerful tool for transformation.

The biggest drains on your emotional power are the issues that lie underneath your anger – issues that you haven't been able to make peace with. They may be things you've rehashed again and again or "accepted" with resignation but without a real sense of resolution or peace. With your heart intelligence you can eliminate resignation and transmute the resistance, numbness, rigidity, insecurity, or even raw fear that resignation might be covering up. It's important to send the power of compassion to those feelings and the neural patterns that hold them. Sending yourself compassion is actualizing deeper care. With deeper care and compassion, it will be easier to Freeze-Frame or slow-frame and see more objectively what's underneath. As you add compassion and slow the frames of feelings and thoughts about whatever happened, you can achieve a new neutral attitude even if your feelings aren't neutral. Practice being neutral about your disturbed feelings. Neutral will give you a window to more objectivity. Then your heart can come in with intuitive insight. Continue to send love and compassion into your disturbance, and you can make the window into a door and walk through to new release.

Slowing it all down is the first step. Going to Neutral to make peace with all of it is the next step. Remember, neutral isn't agreeing with what happened, it's making peace with the fact that it did happen so the past will release its hold on you. That's what *will draw to you the wisdom or understanding that you weren't able to find before.*

The power to forgive comes from your new coherence. Resigning yourself to resentments such as "Things are just that way" or "I know how he'll respond" is a trap laid by your emotional history. Coherence reorganizes your neural circuitry and empowers you to forgive without the old resistances clouding up your thoughts and feelings. It brings closure to the old disturbances. Ask for what you haven't forgiven to be revealed to you, and then use your heart tools until the release is complete, even if it takes ongoing practice and repetition.

"Ask and you shall receive" has been said by philosophers through the ages, but usually there's too much emotional incoherence in the way for people to hear what's there to receive. Address your heart with a deeper wanting to receive more intuitive intelligence and insight from your spirit. Once you gain a new insight, be earnest about anchoring it in your system, not just in your thinking but in your feelings and your actions, so it doesn't fade away. Anchoring is honoring and acting on your heart intuitions until they become part of you.

Heart Technology. Heart rhythm feedback training is a powerful way to refine your use of the heart tools and increase your capacity to sustain emotional coherence. The Institute of HeartMath and Quantum Intech, Inc. have developed technologies that enable heart rhythm coherence to be monitored objectively. One such technology, the Freeze-Framer, is an interactive hardware-software system that monitors and displays your heart rate variability patterns in real time as you practice the heart tools. Using a finger sensor to record the pulse wave, the Freeze-Framer plots changes in your heart rhythm on a beat-to-beat basis. As you practice the techniques, you can readily see and experience the changes in your heart rhythm patterns and identify new reference points that will help you shift into the coherent state. The program also analyzes your heart rhythm patterns and calculates a coherence ratio for each session. Your coherence level is displayed on the computer screen as an accumulated score reflecting your success in playing one of three on-screen games designed to reinforce your emotional coherence skills.

Many people report that using the Freeze-Framer has enabled them to experience greater emotional fulfillment and spiritual connectedness in their day-to-day lives. You can use it on your computer at home or at work. By guiding you in entering and sustaining coherence, the Freeze-Framer helps you quickly *rebuild energy* when your emotional energy has been depleted. It helps you accumulate positive emotional energy to support higher creative capacities, so that you can realize more of your full potential. Most important, it enables you to establish a new internal baseline of coherence so that you function better more of the time—until this increased functioning becomes your norm. You generate and reinforce a physiological state of coherence, and because this coherence has been correlated with increased love, care, compassion, inner harmony, vitality, and flow, the heart rhythm feedback also helps create an inner state that is conducive to spiritual experience (Childre and McCraty 2001).

New Hope

As world events continue to speed up and create uncertainty about the future, it's important to remember that the heart tools, techniques, and technologies are *regulators* of physical, emotional, mental, electromagnetic, and spiritual energies. They are intended to help you stop the whirlwind and quickly regroup your internal energies.

HeartMath is simply a scientifically based and user-friendly way to go deeper into your heart and find an internal source of power that's there waiting to be found.

Everyone has it. It's not religious or nonreligious. It's simply the coherent power of the heart, the power of love. Once harnessed, it will enable you to stop stress, rage, anger, frustration, and irritation. It will allow you to live more from the heart, in alignment with your deeper core values.

Love is what increases emotional maturity and helps you develop intuitive intelligence, allowing you to maintain your balance and poise through challenging times. Love regenerates hope, allowing you to see what the future can be as people shift to deeper care and actualize the core values of the heart. It's already happening. The tools are being used in clinics and hospitals, in corporate boardrooms and customer service centers, in police and fire departments, and in schools. As fifteen-year-old Shante wrote after learning the tools to control anger in her classroom, "I learned a lot about deep heart listening. I learned about appreciating the little things. I learned about caring for other people, and to forgive people, not keep grudges, and not to carry things on, because it adds a lot of stress. With the tools you learn how to accept others' faults and realize that they're only human and no one's perfect, especially not you."

Dare to connect with your heart. Dare to use the tools and see what happens. You will be helping not only yourself and those you love and care about, but also the world in which you live. It's not about being perfect, it's about being genuinely honest with yourself and discovering that you have the power to transform yourself and generate new hope.

appendix

Using HeartMath Tools in Clinical Practice

HeartMath tools are positive emotion-refocusing and emotional restructuring techniques that are being used effectively in clinical practice. The tools are used as interventions, alone or with other therapies, to achieve and reinforce both psychological and physiological improvements. HeartMath tools have been found to greatly facilitate the repatterning of unhealthy emotional responses. The experience of achieving an internal shift that has a powerful effect on feelings and physiology helps patients see that *there is something they can do to help themselves feel better and do better.* They don't have to feel that their well-being is entirely dependent on extrinsic therapeutic aids such as drugs, medical procedures, or continual reliance on a therapist. This can substantially change an individual's attitude toward his or her health challenges, which can play an important part in facilitating the healing process.

It should be emphasized that HeartMath interventions are not intended as a substitute for pharmacological or other medical treatments recommended by a primary care physician or specialist. Through using the heart tools and techniques in conjunction with their treatment plans, patients have frequently been able to reduce or even cease medication under a physician's guidance.

Many physicians and clinicians refer patients to a professional who has been trained and licensed by HeartMath, called a HeartMath One-on-One Provider, or to a HeartMath-sponsored seminar to learn the techniques. Others have found that setting up a program in which the patient reads one of the HeartMath books designed for self-learning is also effective. Asking patients to practice the techniques between sessions and regularly report on their experiences can result in substantial improvements in clinical status. Also, encouraging patients to continue to use the tools even as they begin to feel better can help prevent relapse and often promotes further and lasting benefits.

Many individuals with emotional disorders have become so accustomed to the experience of stress and its consequent emotional and physiological dysregulation that they do not recognize stress as unhealthy. Regularly practicing the Attitude Breathing, Go to Neutral, Heart Lock-In, and Freeze-Frame techniques helps patients develop an intolerance for living in distress, an intolerance they either never had or have long forgotten.

While all the HeartMath tools and techniques are ideal for helping patients develop emotional awareness and intercepting inefficient emotional responses as they happen, the Heart Lock-In technique helps sustain emotional balance and coherence as a norm. It allows a state of coherence to be extended over a longer period of time, and then be more easily accessed when most needed (for example, in the event of an emotional crisis). Because of this, Heart Lock-In practice can "power up" the effectiveness of the other tools. Heart Lock-In also provides a peaceful and pleasurable feeling experience that offers relief from mental and emotional turmoil and tends to instill the desire to use other heart tools more regularly to return to this state.

Using the Freeze-Framer emotional management software to demonstrate the significant physiological shifts that patients are able to achieve by using the techniques can often be a robust means of validation to the patient and a powerful motivator. Many individuals have reported achieving rapid improvements in health problems using the Freeze-Framer technology. Because it is designed as a self-contained educational system that provides all that is needed for individuals to learn and benefit from the HeartMath techniques, this technology is an ideal resource for practitioners who wish to refer patients to a comprehensive and motivating means of self-education.

Health improvements from using the HeartMath tools and technologies have been reported in patients with a wide range of conditions, including anger, anxiety, depression, bipolar disorder, attention deficit/hyperactivity disorder, hypertension, arrhythmia, mitral valve prolapse, diabetes, chronic fatigue, fibromyalgia, asthma, arthritis, and AIDS. Clinical studies and case histories of patients with diverse medical conditions have suggested that the HeartMath techniques can have a rapid and significant positive impact on the quality of life of individuals with chronic illness (Luskin et al. 2002; McCraty, Atkinson, and Lipsenthal 2000). Emotional improvements from using HeartMath techniques can often lead to better compliance with other health management regimens, whether these involve practicing other psychological interventions, taking medications, exercising, or adhering to dietary modifications. Many patients who have incorporated the HeartMath interventions as a regular part of their health management regimen have been surprised to discover the significant impact that managing stress and emotions can have on the level of day-to-day physical discomfort associated with their conditions. Learning to generate heart rhythm coherence and autonomic regulation can especially help with other disorders involving the autonomic nervous system, such as panic disorder, chronic alcohol dependence, multiple sclerosis, hypoglycemia, sleep disorders, premenstrual syndrome, migraines, dizziness, irritable bowel syndrome, coronary disease, and congestive heart failure.

It is very likely that by decreasing stress-induced autonomic arousal and hormonal activation and increasing healthy, balanced patterns of physiological activity, the HeartMath techniques place the body in a state more conducive to healing, thereby supporting and amplifying the effects of other therapeutic interventions.

The analysis of heart rhythm patterns or heart rate variability is being utilized increasingly in a variety of fields of medicine as a noninvasive means to identify patients suffering from autonomic dysfunction and to monitor improvements in autonomic function and balance following therapeutic intervention. Because of the sensitivity of HRV patterns to changes in emotional state, many psychologists utilize heart rhythm monitoring effectively as a "camera on the emotions." This heart technology often proves helpful in identifying feelings, reactions, and emotional triggers that operate at a level below a person's conscious awareness but are nevertheless reflected in physiological patterns and processes. Utilizing the Freeze-Framer software and pulse sensor, continuous monitoring of a client's heart rate variability throughout a therapy session is easily accomplished and can give both therapist and client immediate insight into the client's emotional responses, often enabling a more efficient and effective session.

The Freeze-Framer involves no electrode hook-up and is easy to use in a wide variety of settings (workplaces, homes, or schools). Given its practicality, portability, and low cost, many health-care professionals choose to acquire a number of the systems, which may then be loaned or rented out to patients. This facilitates practice of the heart tools and techniques at home or at work, which can aid clients in sustaining the improvements achieved in therapy sessions. In addition to facilitating the use of the HeartMath techniques, the Freeze-Framer can also be used to monitor and evaluate the psychophysiological effects of other therapeutic interventions (for example, relaxation methods, meditation, controlled breathing, or hypnosis) in real time.

Relaxation, Visualization, and Meditation

The main effect of relaxation, visualization, and meditation interventions is to lower arousal levels (decrease sympathetic activity and increase parasympathetic activity), which may facilitate physical regeneration of the body similar to that which occurs during sleep. Most of these methods focus primarily on the mind and serve as helpful distraction techniques. They can provide respite by redirecting attention to other stimuli and away from the distressing emotion.

The objective of HeartMath interventions is to transform the underlying feeling state that is the *source* of excessive or inappropriate arousal. By generating a positive feeling while simultaneously focusing attention on the heart, HeartMath techniques alter the pattern of cardiac input to the brain. The physiological effects produced are distinct from those associated with the relaxation response. HeartMath techniques have been shown to decrease inappropriate sympathetic activation and increase parasympathetic activity, thus encompassing a key element of the relaxation response (McCraty et al. 1995). However, unlike most relaxation and meditation techniques, HeartMath interventions readily generate characteristic, sustained patterns associated with a shift to the physiological coherence mode, as reflected by smooth, ordered heart rhythms, entrainment of oscillatory systems, system-wide resonance, and increased harmony and synchronization in nervous system and heart-brain dynamics (McCraty and Childre in press). The generation of the coherent mode is a key feature of HeartMath techniques, central to the ability to sustain perceptual and emotional shifts as well as long-term hormonal changes such as an increased DHEA/cortisol ratio, outcomes not necessarily seen with the practice of relaxation or cognitive methods.

With the exception of certain heart-centered meditation and breathing techniques, relaxation, visualization, and meditation techniques rarely lead to increased physiological coherence. It should be noted that although relaxation methods may occasionally induce positive emotions of sufficient duration and amplitude to produce some coherence, these are not consistent outcomes. Moreover, in certain cases, the practice of relaxation and meditation techniques, rather than generating positive emotion, can lead individuals to a state characterized by a degree of ungroundedness and disassociation from life. Such states, if regularly maintained, can actually tend to reduce physiological flexibility and emotional resiliency rather than enhance it. To prevent such outcomes, HeartMath interventions can be used to facilitate and increase the effectiveness of relaxation, visualization, meditation, or other cognitive techniques by helping individuals readily engage and sustain heart-focused positive emotions.

The use of imagery is included in some of the steps of the HeartMath interventions; however, the primary emphasis is on genuinely experiencing a positive *feeling* rather than only calling up a pleasant mental memory or image and visualizing it in the mind's eye. The addition of the emotional shift is critical to the repatterning of the neural circuitry and establishment of a new baseline pattern, which in turn helps determine one's response to future stressors. It is our view that the reason visual imagery works when it does, when used for the purpose of stress or anger management, is not primarily the imagery itself, but rather the positive feelings that the imagery may evoke. The difficulty arises in the fact that suggested imagery may drive quite different emotional responses in two individuals. Therefore, it requires a very skilled practitioner to identify what imagery works for each person.

Alternatively, some therapists keep the imagery vague in the hope that the patient will construct an image that induces a powerful enough positive emotional state to produce a physiological shift. This means that the therapeutic intervention relies on the effective coupling of image and emotion by the subjects themselves. A third approach is to add extensive detail and many sensory modalities to the imagery in the hope that a more detailed image will provoke a more powerful emotion. Such an approach, however, runs the risk of preoccupying the subject with mental processes rather than the emotional processes that are really producing the physiological shifts.

Some practitioners have found it effective to use HeartMath techniques in conjunction with visualization and guided imagery therapies in order to help patients efficiently generate and maintain a genuine heartfelt positive emotional state throughout the visualization process. Such an intervention can often promote a more powerful and enduring psychophysiological shift, leading to desired outcomes.

Many practitioners suggest the use of meditation to facilitate intuitive insights. Most meditative techniques attempt to use the mind to quiet the mind, and therefore can require extensive periods of focused practice to be used effectively. Even those meditation techniques that involve focus in the heart often use the mind to direct the attention, rather than engaging a positive emotion to induce a shift to increased systemic coherence. Many experienced meditators who have learned the HeartMath techniques are surprised at how quickly and easily the interventions lead to an internal state that would commonly require years of meditative practice to achieve.

Adding the HeartMath Interventions

Because the HeartMath techniques can be learned and implemented with minimal time and effort and generally yield immediate, tangible improvements, they have a high rate of patient compliance. By improving emotional self-regulation, the techniques can also help patients increase compliance with other therapies and self-care procedures. Since the interventions directly address and transform the *emotions* at the source of distress, their practice often results in positive changes more rapid and enduring than those generally attainable through many commonly used psychotherapeutic methods or stress management techniques. The interventions can serve as a powerful addition to any biomedical or psychotherapeutic treatment modality, to enhance emotional, mental, and physiological balance and promote systemic healing and recovery. In summary, the advantages of adding HeartMath interventions to other therapeutic practices are as follows:

HeartMath addresses the source of stress. A primary distinguishing feature of HeartMath interventions is that these techniques operate in the emotional domain and focus on directly transforming the negative emotions that are the source of most stress.

HeartMath is easily used in the midst of stress. HeartMath techniques differ from many other stress management strategies in their brevity and adaptability for application during real life situations. Many cognitive therapeutic approaches, meditation and relaxation programs, as well as exercise, fitness, and nutritional education regimens, while beneficial for a healthy lifestyle, require extended blocks of time or a separate space and cannot be utilized when relief from stress is most needed. The simplicity and speed of HeartMath techniques lends them to easy application in virtually any context—in the car, at the dinner table, in the meeting room, or at the workplace. These interventions are designed to meet the immediate needs of contemporary life, and because they can be used in the "heat of battle," are ideal for transforming stress as it arises.

HeartMath is highly generalizable, readily learned, and rapidly effective. Perhaps one of the most compelling aspects of HeartMath interventions is their generalizability among people of diverse cultures, age groups, socioeconomic statuses, and spiritual persuasions. The techniques are free of religious or cultural bias, and can be grasped easily and used effectively and enjoyably by virtually all people. HeartMath techniques are also applicable in the treatment of a wide variety of physical and psychological disorders. The interventions affect virtually all aspects of physiology and provide a viable method of reducing the cumulative emotional energy drains that contribute to the development and progression of many illnesses.

HeartMath has a positive focus. An important benefit of HeartMath interventions is their capacity to assist individuals in achieving therapeutic release without retraumatization. To a large extent, they circumvent the laborious and emotionally painful process of "working through" past issues in order to gain emotional relief, and for this reason also frequently shorten treatment time. The process of reliving painful memories, as often prescribed in some behavioral treatment protocols, can reopen old emotional wounds and actually reinforce unproductive emotional patterns and memories. HeartMath techniques, in contrast, infuse the system with pleasurable, positive emotional experiences which over time create new baseline patterns represented in the neural circuitry and naturally facilitate the release of negative emotional patterns. The interventions instill empowerment and choice, giving each person more control over his or her own experience. This is particularly beneficial for those with a history of trauma who feel like helpless victims.

HeartMath has a high compliance rate. The practicality and ease of application of the techniques, together with the often immediate shifts gained from their use, gives these interventions a notably high rate of compliance. Poor compliance with treatment protocols is a problematic area in both mental health and medical care. Even the best interventions can only be effective to the extent that they are used, and many patients refuse to comply with treatment protocols that are too cognitive, difficult to engage in, or time-consuming; cause them too much physical or emotional discomfort; produce negative side effects; or do not yield positive outcomes in a timely manner. HeartMath techniques allow patients to *feel better* in a way that is tangible to most people. This change can be immediately and objectively validated through heart rhythm monitoring, and the interventions produce no negative side effects. Furthermore, the nature of the interventions enables individuals to continue to use them post-recovery to maintain and enhance health, wellness, and performance. The overall positive experience of using the techniques makes them self-motivating practices to promote health and personal effectiveness.

HeartMath is supportive of other therapies. HeartMath interventions can easily be utilized in conjunction with other treatment modalities—whether pharmaceutical, psychological, or behavioral. Rather than interfere with other therapies, the techniques often enhance the effectiveness of concurrent protocols in a number of ways. First, by reducing inappropriate emotional arousal, the interventions naturally create a more balanced and regenerative physiological environment, as evidenced by direct effects on the immune, nervous, hormonal, and cardiovascular systems. This, in turn, increases receptivity to concurrent therapies. Further, the techniques help instill positive attitudes that may encourage greater adherence to self-care behaviors, thereby supporting other treatment regimens. Thus, the integration of the HeartMath interventions in virtually any therapeutic protocol is likely to speed recovery time and facilitate desired outcomes.

Tips for Using the Techniques in Therapeutic Environments

HeartMath techniques are generally easy to learn, and it is not uncommon for patients to experience positive shifts as soon as they start to use the interventions. However, it is helpful for health care practitioners to utilize the techniques themselves and become familiar with their effects in order to better facilitate patients' growth. It is also important to be aware of several common challenges that can interfere with initial attempts to utilize the techniques effectively.

Focus on imagery rather than feeling. HeartMath interventions were developed and tested for efficacy based upon activating or *feeling* a positive emotional state such as appreciation, care, or love. Therefore, to successfully apply these tools, it is essential to genuinely feel a positive attitude or emotion, as opposed to merely thinking about or recalling a mental image of a happy time or pleasurable experience. Daydreaming, visualizing, wishful thinking, or other cognitive activity alone will not produce the necessary psychophysiological changes conducive to emotion regulation and the establishment of new baseline patterns. The distinction between engaging in positive mental activity and activating a positive emotional state may initially be difficult to grasp, particularly for those who are highly mentally oriented.

Many individuals have success in attaining a genuine positive emotional state by recalling someone they love or an aspect of their present lives that they can sincerely appreciate, and then concentrating on the *feeling* evoked by these positive stimuli. Alternatively, some may choose to focus on the feeling experience associated with special moments or times spent with children, grandchildren, or pets. Some like to reexperience feelings of joy, accomplishment, or contentment associated with events such as successfully completing a special work project, running in a race, or sitting on the beach at dusk and celebrating the sunset. It is important to focus primarily on the *emotional experience,* rather than getting lost in the visualization or cognitive process of reconstructing the details of a positive memory.

Difficulty maintaining heart focus. The practice and sensation of heart focus can be unfamiliar and challenging to some at first. A variety of approaches may be used to learn heart focus. First, focus on the index finger or big toe, and once accustomed to these sensations, shift attention to the area around the heart. Gently placing a hand on the heart is also helpful in directing and sustaining heart focus. In certain circumstances, placing a hand over the heart may draw unwanted attention from others. Touching the heart for just a moment, then breathing slowly and gently through the heart, is also an effective way to help focus attention in that area.

Focus on the mind rather than the heart. Some individuals with prior experience in meditation, visualization, or other mind-focused techniques may be accustomed to a sensation of accumulation of energy in the head area (often around the center of the forehead), and associate this sensation with stress management and wellness practices. With the HeartMath techniques, it is important to focus attention in the heart area instead. It is also important to remain clearheaded and grounded while using HeartMath interventions by periodically breathing through the area around the heart and solar plexus.

"I've tried it and it doesn't work!" Patients may try using one or more of the techniques but claim that they are not experiencing any benefits or have painful memories or feelings come up in the heart area. In these situations, they may need more assistance to get into the coherent heart rhythm mode. One way to objectively assess coherence is to monitor heart rhythms with the Freeze-Framer software while using one of the techniques. However, it should be noted that, on rare occasions, people may experience a genuine positive emotional shift without effecting noticeable changes in heart rhythm. Ultimately, self-report of emotional or perceptual changes remains the best measure of effective use of the techniques.

Learn More about HeartMath

Explore other HeartMath books, learning programs, music, software, seminars, and professional training to reinforce and advance what you've learned in this book. More details can be found online at *www.heartmath.com.*

Books and Learning Programs

Childre, Doc, and Deborah Rozman. 2002. *Overcoming Emotional Chaos: Eliminate Anxiety, Lift Depression and Create Security in Your Life.* San Diego: Jodere Group.

Childre, Doc, and Howard Martin. 1999. *The HeartMath Solution.* San Francisco: HarperSanFrancisco.

Childre, Doc, and Bruce Cryer. 2000. *From Chaos to Coherence: The Power to Change Performance.* Boulder Creek, Calif.: Planetary Publications.

From Chaos to Coherence (CD-ROM). HeartMath LLC: Boulder Creek, Calif. and Knowledgebuilder.com.

Childre, Doc. 1998. *Freeze-Frame: A Scientifically Proven Technique for Clear Decision Making and Improved Health.* Boulder Creek, Calif.: Planetary Publications.

Childre, Doc. 1996. *Teaching Children to Love: 80 Games and Fun Activities for Raising Balanced Children in Unbalanced Times.* Boulder Creek, Calif.: Planetary Publications.

Childre, Doc. 1992. *The How to Book of Teen Self Discovery.* Boulder Creek, Calif.: Planetary Publications.

The HeartMath Method. 2002. Niles, Ill.: Nightingale-Conant. Audio learning series.

Freeze-Frame Learning Program (CD-ROM). Planetary Publications: Boulder Creek, Calif.

Music by Doc Childre

These recordings are scientifically designed to enhance the practice of HeartMath techniques and tools.

Heart Zones. Planetary Publications.

Speed of Balance. Planetary Publications.

Quiet Joy. Planetary Publications.

Freeze-Framer Software

The Freeze-Framer is a patented interactive learning system with a heart rhythm monitor and pulse sensor. This software-based program allows you to observe your heart rhythms in real time and assists you in increasing coherence to improve health and performance.

HeartMath Seminars and Training

HeartMath provides world-class training programs for organizations, hospitals, health-care providers, and individuals. HeartMath training is available through on-site programs for organizations and through sponsored workshops, seminars, and conference presentations.

Licensing and Certification: Training to Become a One-on-One Provider

HeartMath offers licensing and certification to health-care providers, coaches, and consultants wanting to use HeartMath tools and technologies as part of the services they provide to clients in a one-on-one professional model.

Licensing and Certification: "Train the Trainer" Programs for Organizations

HeartMath offers licensing and training to organizations wanting to make the HeartMath tools and technologies a part of their offerings to internal customers, employees, or members.

For information on products, seminars, and workshops, call (800) 450-9111, e-mail *info@heartmath.com,* visit the website at *www.heartmath.com,* or write to: HeartMath, 14700 West Park Avenue, Boulder Creek, CA 95006.

Research and Education

The Institute of HeartMath (IHM) is a nonprofit research and education organization dedicated to understanding emotions and the role of the heart in learning, performance, and well-being. IHM offers programs for use in educational and classroom settings, including:

- *TestEdge* programs for improving academic performance and test scores

- *Resiliency* programs for teachers, administrators, and principals

- *Emotional Security Tool Kit for Children and Teens,* which includes HeartMath techniques to reduce anger, worry, and anxiety, adapted for children ages two to eighteen, available for free at *www.heartmath.org*

For information about Institute of HeartMath research initiatives and education programs, corporate sponsorship, donations, or endowments, please call (831) 338-8500, e-mail *info@heartmath.org,* visit the website at *www.heartmath.org,* or write to: Institute of HeartMath, 14700 West Park Avenue, Boulder Creek, CA 95006.

References

American Heart Association. 2001. *2002 Heart and Stroke Statistical Update.* Dallas: American Heart Association.

Armour, J. A., and J. L. Ardell, eds. 1994. *Neurocardiology.* New York: Oxford University Press.

Associated Press. 2002. Housewife seeking appreciation quits housework. *CNN.com.* www.cnn.com/2002/US/ midwest/10/05/wife.strike.ap [October 5].

Barrios-Choplin, B., R. McCraty, and M. Atkinson. 1999. The effect of employee self-management training on personal and organizational quality. Boulder Creek, Calif.: HeartMath Research Center, Institute of HeartMath. Publication No. 99-083.

Childre, D., and R. McCraty. 2001. Psychophysiological correlates of spiritual experience. *Biofeedback* 29 (4): 13–17.

Clifton, J. K. 2002. Winning business in the emotional economy. *Gallup Management Journal.* www.gmj.gallup.com/ print/?i=209%20 [September 18].

Daniels, C. 2002. The last taboo: It's not sex. It's not drinking. It's stress—and it's soaring. *Fortune,* October 28.

Elbert, T., C. Pantev, C. Wienbruch, B. Rockstroh, and E. Taub. 1995. Increased cortical representation of the fingers of the left hand in string players. *Science* 270 (5234): 305–7.

Ferguson, A. 1998. Road rage. *Time Magazine,* January 12, 44–48.

Frysinger, R. C., and R. M. Harper. 1990. Cardiac and respiratory correlations with unit discharge in epileptic human temporal lobe. *Epilepsia* 31: 162–71.

Gallacher, J. E., J. W. Yarnell, P. M. Sweetnam, P. C. Elwood, and S. A. Stansfeld. 1999. Anger and incident heart disease in the Caerphilly study. *Psychosomatic Medicine* 61 (4): 446–53.

Girardet, E. 1999. Survey: One in four employees feels angry at work. *Associated Press,* Chicago, August 10. Citing D. Gibson and S. Barsade. 1999. The experience of anger at work: Lessons from the chronically angry. Paper presented at the Academy of Management Annual Meeting, August 6–11, Chicago, Ill.

Harris Interactive. 2002. *Tension Tracker 2002: Report of findings.* Fort Washington, Penn.: McNeil Consumer & Specialty Pharmaceuticals.

Huggins, C. E. 2002. Marriage-related anger can hurt wife's health. *Reuters Health,* October 8.

Ironson, G., C. B. Taylor, M. Boltwood, T. Bartzokis, C. Dennis, M. Chesney, S. Spitzer, and G. M. Segall. 1992. Effects of anger on left ventricular ejection fraction in coronary artery disease. *American Journal of Cardiology* 70 (3): 281–85.

Ito, T. A., J. T. Larsen, N. K. Smith, and J. T. Cacioppo. 1998. Negative information weighs more heavily on the brain: The negativity bias in evaluative categorizations. *Journal of Personality and Social Psychology* 75 (4): 887–900.

Kelleher, K. J., T. K. McInerny, W. P. Gardner, G. E. Childs, and R. C. Wasserman. 2000. Increasing identification of psychosocial problems: 1979–1996. *Pediatrics* 105 (6): 1313–21.

King, P. 2002. Why stress tips the scales. *Los Angeles Times,* April 22.

Lacey, J. and B. Lacey. 1970. Some autonomic–central nervous system interrelationships. In *Physiological Correlates of Emotion,* by P. Black. New York: Academic Press.

Lampert, R., S. Baron, C. A. McPherson, and F. A. Lee. 2002. Long-reaching effects of terrorism: Altered heart rate variability during and after September 11, 2001. *Pacing and Clinical Electrophysiology* 25 (4, Part 2): 630.

Luskin, F. 1999. *The effects of forgiveness training on psychosocial factors in college-age adults.* Ph.D. diss., Counseling Psychology, Stanford University.

Luskin, F., M. Reitz, K. Newell, T. G. Quinn, and W. Haskell. 2002. A controlled pilot study of stress management training of elderly patients with congestive heart failure. *Preventive Cardiology* 5 (4): 168–72, 176.

Maccoby, M. 1976. The head and the heart. In *The Gamesman.* New York: Simon and Schuster.

Matthews, K. A., J. F. Owens, L. H. Kuller, K. Sutton-Tyrrell, and L. Jansen-McWilliams. 1998. Are hostility and anxiety associated with carotid atherosclerosis in healthy postmenopausal women? *Psychosomatic Medicine* 60 (5): 633–38.

McCraty, R. 2002. Influence of cardiac afferent input on heart-brain synchronization and cognitive performance. *International Journal of Psychophysiology* 45 (1–2): 72–73.

McCraty, R. Forthcoming. Heart-brain neurodynamics: The making of emotions. In *Emotional Sovereignty,* edited by D. Childre, R. McCraty, and B. C. Wilson. Amsterdam: Harwood Academic Publishers.

McCraty, R. In press. The energetic heart: Bioelectromagnetic communication within and between people. In *Clinical Applications of Bioelectromagnetic Medicine,* edited by P. Rosch and M. Markov. New York: Marcel Dekker.

McCraty, R., M. Atkinson, W. A. Tiller, G. Rein, and A. D. Watkins. 1995. The effects of emotions on short term heart rate variability using power spectrum analysis. *American Journal of Cardiology* 76 (14): 1089–93.

McCraty, R., M. Atkinson, and D. Tomasino. 2001. *Science of the Heart.* Boulder Creek, Calif.: HeartMath Research Center, Institute of HeartMath. Publication No. 01-001.

McCraty, R., M. Atkinson, D. Tomasino, and W. A. Tiller. 1998. The electricity of touch: Detection and measurement of cardiac energy exchange between people. In *Brain and Values: Is a Biological Science of Values Possible,* edited by K. H. Pribram. Mahwah, N.J.: Lawrence Erlbaum Associates, Publishers.

McCraty, R., B. Barrios-Choplin, D. Rozman, M. Atkinson, and A. D. Watkins. 1998. The impact of a new emotional self-management program on stress, emotions, heart rate variability, DHEA and cortisol. *Integrative Physiological and Behavioral Science* 33 (2): 151–70.

McCraty, R., and D. Childre. In press. The grateful heart: The psychophysiology of appreciation. In *The Psychology of Gratitude,* edited by R. A. Emmons and M. E. McCullough. New York: Oxford University Press.

Mittleman, M. A., M. Maclure, J. B. Sherwood, R. P. Mulry, G. H. Tofler, S. C. Jacobs, R. Friedman, H. Benson, and J. E. Muller. 1995. Triggering of acute myocardial infarction onset by episodes of anger. *Circulation* 92 (7): 1720–25.

National Safety Council. 1995. *Stress Management.* Boston: Jones and Bartlett Publishers.

Potter-Efron, R. 1994. *Angry All the Time: An Emergency Guide to Anger Control.* Oakland, Calif.: New Harbinger Publications.

Pribram, K. H. 1991. *Brain and Perception: Holonomy and Structure in Figural Processing.* Hillsdale, N.J.: Lawrence Erlbaum Associates, Publishers.

Pribram, K. H., and F. T. Melges. 1969. Psychophysiological basis of emotion. In *Handbook of Clinical Neurology,* edited by P. J. Vinken and G. W. Bruyn. Amsterdam: North-Holland Publishing Company.

Reaney, P. 2002. Work stress doubles risk of heart disease death. *Reuters,* London, October 17. Citing Kivimäki, M., P. Leino-Arjas, R. Luukkonen, H. Riihimäki, J. Vahtera, and J. Kirjonen. 2002. Work stress and risk of cardiovascular mortality: Prospective cohort study of industrial employees. *British Medical Journal* 325 (7369): 857. www.bmj.com/cgi/content/full/325/7369/857 [October 19].

Rein, G., M. Atkinson, and R. McCraty. 1995. The physiological and psychological effects of compassion and anger. *Journal of Advancement in Medicine* 8 (2): 87–105.

Rosch, P. J. 1997. Working moms—more stress, but worth it. *Health and Stress: The Newsletter of the American Institute of Stress* No. 1: 5–7.

Rosenthal, N. E. 2002. *The Emotional Revolution: How the Science Of Feelings Can Transform Your Life.* New York: Citadel Press.

Schwartz, J. M., and S. Begley. 2002a. *The Mind and the Brain: Neuroplasticity and the Power of Mental Force.* New York: ReganBooks.

Schwartz, J. M., and S. Begley. 2002b. Parts of the brain used most expand, rewire on demand. *Wall Street Journal,* October 11.

Siegman, A. W., S. T. Townsend, R. S. Blumenthal, J. D. Sorkin, and A. C. Civelek. 1998. Dimensions of anger and CHD in men and women: Self-ratings versus spouse ratings. *Journal of Behavioral Medicine* 21 (4): 315–36.

Smith, J. W. 2002. *Dreams interrupted: A year later and beyond.* Chapel Hill, N.C.: Yankelovich, Inc.

Steinberg, J. S., A. Arshad, M. Kowalski, A. Kukar, V. Suma, P. Homel, and A. Rozanski. 2002. The World Trade Center attack: Effect on the occurrence of life-threatening ventricular   arrhythmias.   *Pacing   and   Clinical Electrophysiology* 25 (4, Part 2): 587.

Tiller, W. A., R. McCraty, and M. Atkinson. 1996. Cardiac coherence: A new, noninvasive measure of autonomic nervous system order. *Alternative Therapies in Health and Medicine* 2 (1): 52–65.

Tsuji, H., F. J. Venditti, Jr., E. S. Manders, J. C. Evans, M. G. Larson, C. L. Feldman, and D. Levy. 1994. Reduced heart rate variability and mortality risk in an elderly cohort. The Framingham Heart Study. *Circulation* 90 (2): 878–83.

Umetani, K., D. H. Singer, R. McCraty, and M. Atkinson. 1998. Twenty-four hour time domain heart rate variability and heart rate: Relations to age and gender over nine decades. *Journal of the American College of Cardiology* 31 (3): 593–601.

U.S. Department of Transportation. Cited in Condon, G. 1998. Handling the boiling point: Research challenges commonly held beliefs about anger. *San Jose Mercury News,* July 29.

Doc Childre is the founder and chairman of the scientific advisory board of the Institute of HeartMath, the chairman of HeartMath LLC, and the chairman and CEO of Quantum Intech. He is the author of seven books and a consultant to business leaders, scientists, educators, and the entertainment industry on Intui-Technology®. His HeartMath System and proprietary heart rhythm technology for coherence building, called the *Freeze-Framer®*, has been featured in *The Wall Street Journal, USA Today, Harvard Business Review, Prevention magazine, Psychology Today, Army Times, New York Newsday, Los Angeles Times, San Francisco Chronicle, San Jose Mercury News* and on NBC's *Today Show*, ABC *Good Morning America*, ABC *World News Tonight*, CNN *Headline News*, *CNN.com*, as well as numerous other publications and television programs around the world

He and his coauthor Deborah Rozman, Ph.D., wrote *Overcoming Emotional Chaos*. He also wrote *The How-To-Book of Teen Self-Discovery* and coauthored *The HeartMath Solution* and *From Chaos to Coherence.*

Deborah Rozman, Ph.D., is a psychologist and author with thirty years of experience as an educator and business executive. She is President of Quantum Intech, overseeing strategic alliances and the expansion of HeartMath technologies worldwide. Dr. Rozman is a key spokesperson for the HeartMath system, giving media interviews and keynote addresses on heart intelligence and Intui-Technologies for executives, scientists, and health professionals throughout the world. She is the author of four books and is listed in *Who's Who in California.*

Some Other New Harbinger Titles

Your Depression Map, Item YDM $19.95

Successful Problem Solving, Item SPS $17.95

Working with the Self-Absorbed, Item WSAB $14.95

The Procrastination Workbook, Item PROW $17.95

Coping with Uncertainty, Item COPE $11.95

The BDD Workbook, Item BDDW $18.95

You, Your Relationship, and Your ADD, Item YYY $17.95

The Stop Walking on Eggshells Workbook, Item SWEW $18.95

Conquer Your Critical Inner Voice, Item CYIC $15.95

The PTSD Workbook, Item PWK $17.95

Hypnotize Yourself Out of Pain Now!, Item HYOP $14.95

The Depression Workbook, 2nd edition, Item DWR2 $19.95

Beating the Senior Blues, Item YCBS $17.95

Shared Confinement, Item SDCF $15.95

Handbook of Clinical Psychopharmacology for Therpists, 3rd edition, Item HCP3 $55.95

Getting Your Life Back Together When You Have Schizophrenia Item GYLB $14.95

Do-It-Yourself Eye Movement Technique for Emotional Healing, Item DIYE $13.95

Stop the Anger Now, Item SAGN $17.95

The Self-Esteem Workbook, Item SEWB $18.95

The Habit Change Workbook, Item HBCW $19.95

The Memory Workbook, Item MMWB $18.95

Call **toll free, 1-800-748-6273,** or log on to our online bookstore at **www.newharbinger.com** to order. Have your Visa or Mastercard number ready. Or send a check for the titles you want to New Harbinger Publications, Inc., 5674 Shattuck Ave., Oakland, CA 94609. Include $4.50 for the first book and 75¢ for each additional book, to cover shipping and handling. (California residents please include appropriate sales tax.) Allow two to five weeks for delivery.

Prices subject to change without notice.